BROKENNESS AND BLESSING

D1643261

SARUM THEOLOGICAL LECTURES

BROKENNESS AND BLESSING

Towards a Biblical Spirituality

Frances M. Young

DARTON·LONGMAN+TODD

First published in 2007 by
Darton, Longman and Todd Ltd
1 Spencer Court
140–142 Wandsworth High Street
London SW18 4JJ

ISBN-10: 0–232–52656–7
ISBN-13: 978–0–232–52656–1

A catalogue record is available for this book from the British Library.

Phototypeset by YHT Ltd, London
Printed and bound in Great Britain by
The Cromwell Press, Trowbridge, Wiltshire

CONTENTS

INTRODUCTION

'Towards a Biblical Spirituality – Recovering the Past for the Future' – that title captured the essentials of the project articulated in the Sarum Theological Lectures for 2004. Over years of research, I had learned much about the way the Bible had been used and interpreted by the so-called 'Fathers' of the Church. As a teacher of Biblical Studies, I had operated in a very different way – according to the academic conventions of modernity. As a preacher I had struggled with the gap between the work of biblical scholars and what is practised and believed by faithful church-goers. The invitation to deliver the Sarum Theological Lectures provided an opportunity for me to try and address the questions raised not only by that gap but also by the current tensions around Scripture that cross the denominations, and to do so by seeking a renewal of biblical spirituality through learning from past Christian teachers.

The lectures thus drew upon a long-standing research interest in a context that demanded engagement with contemporary church life and spirituality. My idea was that exploring the ways in which the earliest theologians and preachers read the Bible would enable us to follow their approach, not necessarily adopting all their conclusions, but certainly reopening the question whether the 'spiritual meaning' of the text may not be more important than the 'literal' or 'historical' meaning. In seeking contemporary applications, the lectures drew on reflections on current global issues, but also on personal experiences.

It was always my intention to refer to the L'Arche communities, from which I have learned much. In L'Arche people commit themselves to living in community with those who have learning disabilities. Founded by Jean Vanier, these communities are now spread all over the world. Originally in the French Roman Catholic tradition, they now have, in the Federation, communities which are ecumenical, and in some parts of the world, multi-faith.

In the event, however, when I should have been preparing the lectures I was in fact distracted by my husband's prostate cancer, so that in delivery they were a rushed job! A year later, as I began to develop them and write them up, my 94-year-old mother was slowly sinking after a massive stroke and the trauma of moving to a nursing home. Despite years of coming to terms with the pre-natal developmental failure of my first-born son, whom we still support at home as he nears 40 years of age, I was continually reminded how profoundly difficult it is to live with our vul-nerability and mortality – how we question and rebel, as we are overwhelmed by grief and distress. The biblical spirituality which emerged from the project challenges the culture we have assimilated, and its assumptions and values, while offering both a realistic view of the human condition and the wonderful gift of grace which brings hope of transformation. It is this conversion of heart which constitutes the purpose of Scripture, according to the Fathers.

Many of our well-known hymns in fact pick up the same kind of spiritual reading of Scripture as we find in the Fathers. For this reason each lecture began with a hymn related to its theme, and these hymns will be found at the head of each chapter in this book. In this way we can see how we already have access to this biblical spirituality, and so we may find the Fathers less strange than we might have supposed. Because we are drawing on this material, Scripture will not be consistently quoted from a modern translation, but more arbitrarily in ways that reflect the meaning and usage of the hymn-writer or the Fathers.

The Fathers may be described as the early theologians of Christianity, dating roughly from the second century to the early medieval period. They include bishops, pastors and preachers, as well as philosophers and intellectuals, scholars and thinkers. The body of literature that has been passed down over the centuries comprises letters, treatises, apologetics, commentaries, homilies, dialogues, polemics, histories, and many other writings.[1] Clearly, it is necessary to provide some information about the people whose work will be exploited, and about some terms that will be used which are not in common usage. The rest of this introduction will consolidate the information that was given to the lecture audience through the medium of hand-outs. It is intended to be useful rather than daunting! The reader is urged not to wade through these lists at the start, but to consult this material as the chapters are read. For this reason the material has been reorganised into alphabetical lists, and only includes those individuals who are actually mentioned and those words that are actually used. Apart from the Fathers, reference is also made to certain Greek philosophers, as well as to one of the most famous of Jewish Rabbis. They are included in the list below.

The Fathers and others

Abba (= Father) John the Persian: a character who appears in the *Apophthegmata Patrum*, the collection of the anecdotes and teachings of the famous ascetics known as the Desert Fathers. They come from approximately the fifth to the eighth centuries.

Ambrose: bishop of Milan in the late fourth century; a politician and pastor, and author of many books in Latin. His preaching contributed to the conversion of **Augustine** (see below).

Amma (= Mother) Theodora: cf. **Abba John the Persian** (see above).

Antony: traditionally the founder of Egyptian monasticism. His *Life* was written by Athanasius.

Apostolic Constitutions: a compendium of works concerning Church order, compiled in the fourth century but containing earlier material, and attributed to the Apostles.

Apostolic Fathers: the term given to the earliest writings other than the New Testament (i.e. the canonical books) – some, such as *The Shepherd of Hermas* and 1 *Clement*, were regarded as part of the canon in the third century (see further below; see also **Ignatius** and **Polycarp**).

Aqiba: one of the earliest of the Jewish Rabbis (end of first century CE). He was present at the Synod of Jamnia, which began the consolidation of Judaism after the destruction of the Temple in 70 CE.

Athanasius: bishop of Alexandria in the fourth century, a prolific author and defender of the faith against the heresy (Arianism) that provoked the promulgation of the Nicene Creed in 325 CE.

Augustine: bishop of Hippo in North Africa at the turn of the fourth and fifth centuries; author of the *Confessions* and other ground-breaking works in Latin, which profoundly influenced the course of Western theology, especially in the Middle Ages and at the Reformation. His work *The City of God* (discussed in Chapter 4) mentions the Christian emperors Constantine (the first to patronise Christianity, in the early fourth century) and Theodosius (ruled in the late fourth century). His less well-known *Enarrationes in Psalmos* ('Explanations of the Psalms', discussed in Chapter 5) is in fact his largest work. He refers the meaning of the Psalms to Christ and to his body, the Church, so that the Psalms become both an articulation of salvation and an expression of praise.

Basil of Caesarea: one of the Cappadocian Fathers (see **Gregory of Nazianzus** below). One of the Eastern Orthodox liturgies still in use purports to go back to Basil.

1 Clement: an epistle written in the late first century by Clement, the bishop (or perhaps the secretary) of the church at Rome, to the Corinthian church. It is counted among the so-called **Apostolic Fathers** and is included in some early lists of canonical books.

Clement of Alexandria (in Egypt): a scholar of the third century, probably the teacher of **Origen** (see below).

Cyril of Alexandria: the patriarch of Egypt in the early fifth century and a protagonist in the controversy about Christ which produced the 'Chalcedonian Definition' in 451 CE. This Definition is taken to encapsulate orthodox doctrine about the person of Christ by all mainstream Christian denominations.

Cyril of Jerusalem: bishop of Jerusalem in the mid fourth century, known for his *Catechetical Homilies*, delivered through Lent to prepare people for baptism on Easter eve.

Donatists: a sizeable North African sect that claimed to be the true, pure Church in that region after refusing to accept bishops who, they claimed, had handed over the Scriptures to the authorities during persecution. The Catholics named them after a leading priest, Donatus. They were a considerable challenge to Augustine.

Ephrem the Syrian: a poet and theologian of the fourth century, who wrote in Syriac. Some of his works are available in English in a volume of the *Classics of Western Spirituality*.

Epistle to Diognetus: the author is an unknown apologist of the second century, and his work is usually to be found among the **Apostolic Fathers**.

Eusebius of Caesarea (in Palestine): the first historian of the Church. A prolific author and apologist, he lived to see Constantine conquer the Eastern Empire, end persecution and patronise Christianity (early fourth century).

Gregory of Nazianzus: one of the fourth-century Cappadocian Fathers (Cappadocia is in modern Turkey). He was the friend of **Basil of Caesarea** and Basil was the brother of **Gregory of Nyssa** (see below). Gregory of Nazianzus is known as 'the theologian' in the Eastern Orthodox churches. His Five Theological Orations were delivered in Constantinople in about 380 CE and are thought to sum up theological orthodoxy.

Gregory of Nyssa: also one of the fourth-century Cappadocian Fathers (see the previous Gregory!). Author of many works and often treated as the first Christian mystic. Influenced by **Origen**.

Helena: mother of Constantine, the first Christian emperor (early fourth century).

Hilary of Poitiers (France): fourth-century bishop who defended Nicene orthodoxy against the Arian heresy in the West, as **Athanasius** did in the East.

Ignatius: bishop of Antioch in the early second century. His seven letters, written on his journey to Rome, where he would suffer martyrdom, are among the earliest Christian texts outside the New Testament and are included among the **Apostolic Fathers**.

Irenaeus: bishop of Lyons at the end of the second century. His works include a large treatise, *Against the Heresies* and a smaller book, *The Demonstration of the Apostolic Preaching*. He is often regarded as the first systematic theologian, though actually he hammered out a defence of what he thought was tradition against heretical ideas.

Jerome: a prolific author in Latin, and translator of the Vulgate. He lived an ascetic life in a monastery in Bethlehem for 30 years up to 420 CE.

John Chrysostom: bishop of Antioch and then Constantinople in the late fourth century. The greatest preacher of the ancient Church. His nickname 'Chrysostom' means 'Golden-mouth'. There survive series of homilies on many books of the Bible, as well as many occasional sermons and other works, often taken down by stenographers when they were delivered.

Justin Martyr: one of the second-century apologists who wrote in defence of Christianity, often addressing their treatises to the emperors. Justin also wrote the *Dialogue with Trypho*, which purports to be a discussion with a Jew on the inter-pretation of what Christians would call the Old Testament.

Leo the Great: bishop of Rome 440–61 CE.

Macarius: a famous fourth-century ascetic of the Egyptian desert, known as 'the Great'.

Macarian Homilies: attributed to Macarius the Great but actually anonymous, almost certainly deriving from Syria. Very influential in Eastern Orthodox monasticism and theology. Discovered by Protestant pietists and translated into German and English in the eighteenth century; published for his preachers by John Wesley. Available in English in the *Classics of Western Spirituality*.

Manichees: followers of Manes, a Persian religious leader of the third century. His teaching is profoundly dualistic, as was the ancient Zoroastrian religion of Persia. Like the Gnostics, he drew on a wide range of different religious traditions, including Christian heretical ideas. His understanding of Christ was assumed to be of a docetic character.

Marcionites: followers of Marcion, a Christian of the second century who rejected the 'Old Testament', thinking that the God of love revealed by Jesus could not be the same as the God of judgement found in the Jewish Scriptures. He seems to have many dualistic ideas in common with the Gnostics, and was assumed to have docetic views about the person of Christ.

Maximus of Tyre: a pagan philosopher of the early Christian era, whose work gives some insight into the intellectual context within which the Fathers did their thinking.

Origen: the first commentator on most of the books of the Bible; a famous third-century teacher in Alexandria and Caesarea, where he founded a library that was inherited by **Eusebius** (see above). He also wrote (about 248 CE) a long refutation of an earlier anti-Christian work by Celsus, written c. 177–80 CE. Origen's work had a profound influence on Eastern theology, though his teaching later became controversial and was retrospectively condemned in the fourth and fifth centuries.

Plato: the great Greek philosopher of the fourth century BCE whose work set the intellectual horizons within which many of the Fathers construed reality.

Polycarp: bishop of Smyrna; contemporary with Ignatius, one of whose letters is addressed to him; was martyred at the age of 86. The story of his death is the earliest martyrdom account that we have.

Tertullian: the first Christian to write in Latin; lived in Carthage, North Africa, in the third century. He wrote many treatises on ethical issues and against heresies.

Theophilus: bishop of Antioch in the second century; like **Justin**, an apologist.

Xenophanes: a pre-Socratic Greek philosopher of the fifth century BCE. Many of the fragments of his work were preserved by the Christian scholar, **Clement of Alexandria** (see above).

Glossary

Agōn: struggle, combat, contest. The word in Greek referred to any sporting event, e.g. a race or wrestling match. It is used metaphorically in the New Testament and the Fathers to refer to the struggle undertaken by the athlete for Christ.

Anagogy/anagogic: these words (abstract noun and corresponding adjective) refer to the 'ascent' that has to be made from what is creaturely, but good or beautiful or true, to the truly Good, Beautiful and True. Earthly signs or symbols have to be 'stretched' beyond creaturely concepts to give a hint of the transcendent.

Apophatic theology: theology that proceeds on the basis of distinguishing God from everything created, and so focusing on negative adjectives such as immortal, invisible, incorporeal, infinite, indefinable, incomprehensible, impassible, etc.

Aporia: something that leaves you at a loss – a difficulty you cannot resolve, a concept you cannot conceive, a puzzle!

Aseity: an abstract noun formed from *a se* (Latin) = 'of him/herself'. It expresses the nature of the divine as beyond dependence on anything else – simply being itself of itself.

Docetic: from a Greek word meaning 'seeming' – used in relation to an early heresy which claimed that the Christ only seemed to be human, or simply came onto the human Jesus at baptism and departed before the crucifixion.

Doxa: glory, reputation. Striving for *doxa* was very important in the Greek world. The word was used to translate a Hebrew word which had rather different associations in the Bible, namely the 'glory' of God – often understood as the dazzling light that accompanied theophanies (appearances of the divine) such as that which occurred at the Transfiguration. This shifted Christian perception as to where true *doxa* is to be found – it comes from God's grace, not human achievement.

Encrateia: self-discipline and restraint, especially with respect to sexual continence.

Enoptics: Origen's term, roughly corresponding to metaphysics, but about insight into, specifically, the higher realities behind the physical world.

Epektasis: the state of stretching forward/upward – an abstract term coined by **Gregory of Nyssa** from a verb used in Philippians 3:13.

Eschaton: Greek for 'end', used in English to refer to the ultimate end – God's final purposes as the world ends and the kingdom is established. From this we get 'eschatology' – the doctrines concerning God's ultimate purposes.

Exemplars/'types': people who are models or examples of a particular virtue or way of life. A 'figural reading' of Scripture focuses (a) on such 'figures' as patterns enabling the reader to enter the text and live it, or (b) on models, patterns or stories of the Old Testament as prefiguring or prophesying Christ, the Church or God's future kingdom.

Gēr (pl. gērim): Hebrew word for 'sojourner' or 'resident alien'.

Gnostics: a term used for a variety of different sects (usually known by their founder's name, e.g. Valentinians after Valentinus) which had certain common features. They are treated by the majority of modern scholars as belonging to a single movement, which had pagan, Jewish and Christian forms. Generally they thought that the material creation was the result of a pre-cosmic 'fall' or mistake, and that salvation was escape to the spiritual realm, a privilege for those 'in the know' (N.B.: the Greek word *gnōsis* means 'knowledge' –

hence the term 'Gnostic'). Gnostics thought that everything had issued from the *Bythos* ('the Deep'), a way of expressing the infinity of the ultimate. From the *Bythos* came the *Aeons* (eternal beings, ages or worlds) who made up the *Plerōma* (the fullness of the divine realm).

Hermeneutic: comes from the Greek word for 'translation' and 'interpretation'. It has become a technical term for the way in which a person or community makes sense of the world and/ or a key text such as the Bible.

Hexaēmeron: the Greek word for 'six days', usually referring specifically to the Six Days of Creation.

Ipsissima verba: a Latin term used by scholars to refer to the search for the 'very own words' of Jesus, i.e. his authentic sayings.

Katabasis/katabatic: these words (abstract noun and corresponding adjective) refer to God's 'descent' in revelation and incarnation, whereby knowledge of God is imparted to those who are willing to receive in humility.

Katharsis: Aristotle, a fourth-century BCE Greek philosopher, wrote about tragedy in his *Poetics*. He suggested that tragedy effects *katharsis* by provoking pity and fear. The word means 'purification'. Since tragic drama developed in the context of a religious festival in classical Athens, I would argue that 'purification' retains its religious significance, and that tragic story/drama may have the same kind of 'purifying' effect as sacrifice.

Kenōsis = 'emptying' – a word derived from the celebration of Christ's self-emptying in Philippians 2:5–11.

Logos = 'Word'. Basically meaning anything said, it could be used for a discrete word, or a statement, or an argument, or even reason in the mind before speech. The term was commonly used in philosophy to refer to the rationality which humanity shares with the divine. It is used in the Greek Bible for the 'Word of the Lord' which came to the prophets, and famously in the Prologue to John's Gospel, for the Word incarnate in Jesus.

Brokenness and Blessing

Mephibōsheth = 'son of Jonathan'; also known as 'Meribaal' in the books of Chronicles. 'Baal' = 'Lord/Master', but the word came to be associated, in much of the Old Testament, with the local fertility gods, i.e. false gods over against Israel's Lord God. It is likely that 'Meribaal' was the original name, but when it became unacceptable to use 'Baal', the name was changed to a compound replacing *baal* with *bōsheth*, the Hebrew word for 'shame'.

Mimetic: from the Greek word *mimēsis* (= 'imitation', 'representation'), used for the way drama imitates life; or the way heroes/saints may be exemplary and so worth imitating in life; or the way the Eucharist re-presents the passion of Christ.

Paidagōgos: literally, the slave employed to take a child to school and supervise his work; also the title of a work by **Clement of Alexandria** which focuses on God and his word as the 'tutor' or 'instructor' of the soul.

Panegyrics: praise-speeches.

Paroikos: the Greek equivalent of *gēr* (see above).

Philanthrōpia: love towards humanity; a favourite word in the preaching of John Chrysostom.

Skopos: the 'intent' of an author. The Fathers would enquire into the *skopos* of the Holy Spirit in Scripture, thus seeking to grasp the 'scope' of the whole Bible, but also seeking the thrust of individual problematic texts in the light of that.

Stigmata: the wounds of Christ; cf. the tradition that they appeared on the body of St Francis of Assisi.

'Typology': another term for 'figural reading'. See above, **Exemplars/'types'**.

THE DESERT EXPERIENCE

Guide me, O thou great Jehovah,
Pilgrim through this barren land;
I am weak, but thou art mighty;
Hold me by thy powerful hand;
Bread of heaven,
Feed me now and evermore.

Open thou the crystal fountain,
Whence the healing stream shall
    flow;
Let the fiery, cloudy pillar
Lead me all my journey through:
Strong Deliverer,
Be thou still my strength and
    shield.

When I tread the verge of Jordan,
Bid my anxious fears subside;
Death of death, and hell's destruction,
Land me safe on Canaan's side:
Songs of praises
I will ever give to thee.

In this well-known eighteenth-century hymn, we easily recognise allusions to incidents in the Exodus narrative: the manna, the
water from the rock, the pillar of fire by night and the pillar of
cloud by day. Here these motifs become metaphors illuminating
each person's life-pilgrimage. Thus the hymn provides a telling
example of the classic reading of Scripture by which it provides
'types' of the life that each one of us has to live. The way that
people understood their own lives was once shaped by patterns
and models found in Scripture, and conversely, people read their
own lives into Scripture.

   The purpose of this chapter is to demonstrate that this kind of
'typology' is how the Bible has traditionally functioned, thus
producing a biblical spirituality which was carried in liturgy and
hymnography, as well as in private devotion and Scripture

reading. This was the case from the beginning: it is already there in the New Testament writings; it was developed in the theology of the Fathers of the Church. We shall explore some examples from this Christian past, focusing on the motif of the desert-experience; but we shall also consider why it is important self-consciously to reclaim this tradition in our post-modern world, and how it might enable us to approach the Bible more imaginatively and creatively, so as to find it a resource for living in the troubled world of the early twenty-first century.

1. The desert motif in the Bible and the early Church

Inner-biblical interpretation

An obvious appeal to the story of the Exodus occurs in Psalm 95 (once regularly used in Anglican worship as the *Venite* of the traditional Mattins in the Book of Common Prayer). The wor-shippers who chant the psalm are exhorted not to harden their hearts today as their fathers did in the days of temptation in the wilderness. Already then in the Psalter, the memory of the Exodus becomes a warning to each generation – it has a present reality, rather than just being an event in the past.

This perspective is drawn out in the New Testament as this psalm is taken over by the author of the Epistle to the Hebrews. The words of verses 7–11 are quoted in full, and then the author adds his own exhortation: 'Take care, brothers and sisters, that none of you may have an evil, unbelieving heart that turns away from the living God' (Heb. 3:12). He goes on to insist that that response is required now – 'Today' means 'Today' every day! Always it is possible to lose the promise if you are not careful, and so fail to enter into the rest that God has prepared. This 'rest' becomes more than the Promised Land, for it is taken to represent God's kingdom, the *eschaton*, heaven. The pattern of the whole of history is implied, for God's rest on the seventh day symbolises this 'end' – God's ultimate purposes. The author worries about the possibility of Christians failing through disobedience, even though he is sure that, for the people of God who persevere to the end, a Sabbath rest still remains. Thus even within the Bible, the importance of the story is not what happened in the past, but the way it functions in a new situation, as encouragement or warning for 'Today'.

The desert monks

The prophets sometimes suggested that comfortable Israel needed to return to the desert, and such a return became literalised in the world of the early Church. Tradition makes St Antony the first to have crossed the line from settled land to wilderness. The tale is told that Antony wandered into a church just as the Gospel was being read, and heard the Lord saying to the rich man, 'If you would be perfect, go, sell what you possess and give it to the poor, and you will have treasure in heaven' (Matt. 19:21). His literal response was to sell his inheritance and withdraw into the desert. The story of his ascetic exploits was celebrated in *The Life of Antony*, attributed to Athanasius, a work which had enormous influence on the development of ascetic and monastic practices in both the East and the West. Soon the desert became 'a city'[1] as more and more people rejected civilisation, and a new way of Christian discipleship was celebrated in collections of stories and sayings from the desert fathers.

Some years ago I was flying over Egypt and, looking down, I could see that sharp defining line which differentiates the cultivated Nile valley and the desert on either side of it. I realised more than ever before what stepping across that boundary meant.

For the early ascetics the desert was a place of trial and temptation – as for the Israelites, and as for Jesus. There they found their inner demons exposed: fear and insecurity, anger and violence, self-deception and self-hatred. Let one rather amusing example suffice:

A certain brother while he was in the community was restless and frequently moved to wrath. And he said within himself, 'I shall go and live some place in solitude: and when I have no one to speak to or to hear, I shall be at peace and this passion of anger will be stilled.' So he went forth and lived by himself in a cave. One day he filled a jug for himself with water and set it on the ground, but it happened that it suddenly overturned. He filled it a second time, and again it overturned: and he filled it a third time and set it down, and it overturned again. And in a rage he caught up the jug and broke it. Then when he had come to himself, he thought how he had been tricked by the spirit of anger and said, 'Behold, here am I alone, and nevertheless he hath conquered me. I shall return to the community, for in all places there is need for struggle and for patience and above all for the help of God.' And he arose and returned to his place.[2]

The monks felt they were engaged in battles with the devil, just as Christ had been. They saw their role as engaging in a 'mopping-up operation', Christ having already achieved the victory in principle.[3] They were 'filling up what was lacking in the sufferings of Christ' (Col. 1:24), contending with the powers of evil on behalf of the whole Church, even the whole world.

The practice of renunciation constituted the fight against desire and temptation, a fight which necessitated detachment from possessions. A saying attributed to Amma Theodora goes like this: 'Just as the trees, if they have not stood before the winter's storms, cannot bear fruit, so it is with us; this present age is a storm and without many trials and temptations we cannot obtain an inheritance in the kingdom of heaven.'[4] Temptation was inseparable from experience, and was a good thing, enabling discernment of spirits, and endurance. It produced freedom – it meant not being anxious or worried, and a willingness to move on and venture into unknown territory.

Yet the desert was not just a place of struggle. It was also the place where you met God, where you received wisdom. One saying went, 'Renounce this life so that you may be alive to God.'[5] They looked for holiness and intimacy with God. It was through deep identification with scriptural motifs that they acquired authority, and a kind of prophetic insight into the state of society. They lived out a desert hermeneutic, as their lives were modelled on Scripture, and their reading of it reflected the issues arising in desert life and the world around them. Many were illiterate, but regularly they recited the Psalms by heart. They heard the Scriptures read and were absorbed into the world of the texts. They recognised the power of the word, resisting demonic temptations by scriptural quotation, as Jesus had; 'they felt themselves recapitulating the experience of Jesus',[6] and the motif of 40 days of solitude in the wilderness is repeatedly found in the records. They wanted to fulfil all the commandments, thus 'doing the word'. As Douglas Burton-Christie comments, 'the desert monks took seriously the ethical commitment required for understanding the biblical texts'.[7] Macarius is reported to have said: 'Meditate on the Gospel and the other scriptures, and if a distracting thought arises within you, never look at it but always look upwards, and the Lord will come at once to your help.'[8]

The characters of the Bible provided exemplars. Abba John the Persian, in reply to the question whether the monks would inherit the kingdom after enduring so many afflictions in the desert, said: 'I have been hospitable like Abraham, a hermit like John, filled with repentant sorrow like Jeremiah, a master like Paul, full of faith like Peter, wise like Solomon – so like the thief [crucified with Jesus] I trust that he who of his natural goodness has given me all that, will also grant me the kingdom.'[9] Jesus Christ was the paramount model, however, especially of the virtue of humility. They wanted to imitate his *kenōsis* (self-emptying): 'Obedience is the best ornament of the monk. He who has acquired it will be heard by God, and he will stand beside the crucified with confidence, for the crucified became obedient unto death' (see Phil. 2:8).[10] Humility was to be achieved by the endurance of trials for the sake of Christ; that was the way to be blessed (Matt. 5:10ff). Indeed, the whole purpose of life in the desert is summed up in the Beatitudes creatively re-minted: 'Happy is the monk who thinks he is the offscouring of all' (cf. 1 Cor. 4:13).[11] Thus the Gospel and the whole of Scripture was interpreted through a literal living-out of the desert motif.

The model for the spiritual life

The desert motif was not only played out literally, but also functioned metaphorically as a symbol of the spiritual life. Probably the clearest example is Gregory of Nyssa's *Life of Moses*. Gregory intended his exposition of the scriptural story to provide a pattern of life, possibly for a priest, though this is not explicitly stated. The work illustrates the principle of typology or 'figural reading' – the way the biblical narrative shapes a sense of the Christian life. Gregory's theme is perfection and its attainment.[12]

Perfection in this world needs 'boundaries'. This was a fundamental classical idea. Chaos is not beautiful – rather, beauty is found in the perfect shape of a statue or other artefact. Perfection requires defining limits. But, says Gregory, virtue is not like that.[13] Like the nature of the infinite God, perfection is boundless, and there is no stopping-place or final attainment. Human perfection is always growth in goodness. Moses' life provides a pattern: through contemplation of it we can reach some understanding of what the perfect life might be like, by treating it as a kind of map or guide to the spiritual journey.

Indeed, *journey* is the operative word. Gregory's summary presentation[14] goes something like this: The life of Moses was characterised by journeying, by watching the mysterious cloud that guided the people, teaching them to keep it in sight. Food appeared miraculously, enemies were overcome. At Mount Sinai he and the people were initiated into the divine mysteries, passing through purification to revelation. Moses had to ascend beyond the visible and enter the inner sanctuary of divine mystical doctrine. In subsequent books Gregory ponders the details.

Moses' life is a series of ascending steps up Jacob's ladder, as it were.[15] Proper lifestyle is as important as correct doctrine, both constituting necessary pursuits for true virtue.[16] Purification is spelt out in terms of the ideals of that asceticism which also informed the practice of contemporary desert monks: self-control and austerity of life must accompany developing spirituality; and spirituality is a constant deepening of theological understanding which shapes the heart of one's life and worship. If at first religious knowledge comes as light, further progress and deeper penetration discovers the invisible and the incomprehensible, the darkness in which seeing consists in not seeing, for no one shall see God and live (Exod. 33:20).[17] Then, later, Moses enters the luminous darkness of the cloud of the presence.[18] Transformed by God's glory so that no one can look at him (he has to veil his face, according to Exod. 34:29–35), he speaks with God face to face as one speaks with a friend (Exod. 33:11). Yet to see God is not attainable – God hides him in a cleft of rock, allowing him to see only his back-parts (Exod. 33:22–23). For 'truly this is the vision of God: never to be satisfied in the desire to see him.'[19] Moses is taught how he can behold him – simply by following God wherever he might lead, keeping the back of his leader in view and not turning aside.[20]

Elsewhere, in an important anti-heretical work,[21] another biblical narrative provides Gregory with the basis for his vision of the spiritual life as a journey into the unknown. He describes the saving faith of Abraham, who went out by divine command from his own land on an 'exodus'; leaving behind his lowly, earthly mind, he raised his conception beyond the boundaries of nature, walking by faith, not sight, like the Apostle; lifted so high by his knowledge that he became the model of human perfection, knowing as much of God as it was possible for finite human capacity to attain. Hence God is called the God of Abraham. Abraham outstripped every conception of God, purged his reason of earth-bound images and recognised that God is bigger than anything we can conceive. Purification of heart involves stripping away unworthy mental conceptions, which are idols. The absolute transcendence of the divine must be recognised – otherwise we reduce God to the size of our own minds. The infinity of God implies the incomprehensibility of the divine being.

So it was, says Gregory, that 'Moses' vision of God began with light; afterwards God spoke to him in a cloud. But when Moses rose higher and became more perfect, he saw God in the darkness.'[22] The meaning of Moses' entering the cloud is that, as the soul makes progress, it penetrates deeper and deeper into the invisible and the incomprehensible, and it is there that it sees God. The true vision and the true knowledge of what we seek consists precisely in not seeing, in an awareness that our goal transcends all knowledge and is everywhere cut off from us by the darkness of incomprehensibility. Thus that profound evangelist, John, who penetrated into this luminous darkness, tells us that 'no one has seen God at any time', teaching us by this negation that none – indeed, no created intellect – can attain a knowledge of God.[23]

Repeatedly in Gregory, we find imagery drawn from the sense of climbing a mountain, notably the sense of vertigo when you stand on the top of a cliff and stare down into a bottomless chasm. He asks, What would it be like to put your foot on the edge and find no solid footing? This is what the soul experiences when it goes beyond its footing in material things in its quest for what has no dimension and exists for all eternity – for here there is nothing to take hold of, and so the soul keeps slipping from what cannot be grasped, becoming dizzy and perplexed.[24]

It is as though we struggle up a steep slope to the ridge ahead, and arrive at a stage in perfection; we pause, stand over a cliff and feel the vertigo that comes with the realisation of God's incomprehensibility; and then the clouds ahead part and we see another ridge to climb. There has to be eternal progress, because it is not possible to comprehend or grasp the infinite. Furthermore, change is constitutive of creaturely being – 'our nature is essentially changeable'; since it is made out of nothing, it came into being by change.[25] 'Now to be subject to change is, in a sense, constantly to be born again.'[26] So, for Gregory, the important thing about change is that it is the necessary condition for being 'transformed from glory to glory' (2 Cor. 3:18):

In truth the finest aspect of our mutability is the possibility of growth in good; and this capacity for improvement transforms the soul, as it changes, more and more into the divine ... [So] let us change in such a way that we constantly evolve towards what is better ... thus always improving and ever becoming more perfect by daily growth, and never arriving at any limit of perfection. For perfection consists in our never stopping in our growth in good, never circumscribing our perfection by any limitation.[27]

On the basis of Philippians 3:13, Gregory coined the word *epektasis* to express a sense of straining forward on the upward climb that never stops: 'Moses, moving ever forwards, did not stop in his upward climb.' Abraham too stretched himself forward, constantly transcending what he had so far grasped. Each stage of glory is overtaken by another, and 'no matter how great or sublime it may be, we always believe it to be less than what we hope for.' 'The new grace we may obtain is greater than what we had before', but 'it does not put a limit on our final goal.'[28]

So no limit can be set to our progress towards God: first of all, because no limitation can be put upon the beautiful, and secondly because the increase in our desire for the beautiful cannot be stopped by any sense of satisfaction.[29]

The question for us is whether this is all to be dismissed as allegory, or whether it provides an important model of creatively appropriating the Bible, as its narratives, images and metaphors run together to illuminate our lives. But before we consider that, we need to pursue one more exploration of the use of the desert motif in the early Church.

The redemptive journey

The over-arching story of the Bible was presented in terms of the desert motif, the Exodus being the guiding metaphor. Egypt stands for the world, with all its security and comfort, the desert for escape from the oppressions of the world, from being enslaved to material things and the desires they stimulate. The desert journey represents the stripping down and training of the athlete for Christ, and an anticipation of the restoration of Paradise. So going down into Egypt and then escaping into the desert was assimilated to the grand narrative of Fall and Redemption.

A couple of examples can illustrate this: firstly, the work called *On Worship in Spirit and Truth* written by Cyril of Alexandria.[30] The work is really an interpretation of the five books of Moses in the form of a dialogue, but it begins with a problem, namely: How is Matthew's text, 'not a jot or tittle of the Law will pass away' (Matt. 5:18), to be reconciled with the Johannine saying that the Father will be worshipped not in Jerusalem, but in spirit and in truth (John 4:21–24)? Cyril works through the Law (that is, the Torah or the five books of Moses) to show that it is a 'type' or foreshadowing of the proper shaping of devotion to God. He is convinced that the beauty of truth is hidden within it. The stories and pictures in the Law are to be understood spiritually. The Law acts pedagogically, educating infants and leading them to maturity.

The movement from the Fall into sin, through repentance, to renewal through God's grace becomes a universal paradigm, traced out in one biblical narrative after another, and then applied to 'us' – for each of us are instances of the universal story of the human race. What happened to Adam happens to each of us, says Cyril. Abraham becomes the first exemplar of this truth. Abraham is caught in Egypt by Pharaoh because of Sarah's beauty – he is spiritually enslaved. Pharaoh stands for the father of sin, who treats us well as long as he can distract us with pleasure. Only God and divine grace could rescue Abraham. Jacob, like Abraham, goes to Egypt because of famine, and Israel suffers under the yoke of slavery. The point is that we are called, like Abraham, to follow God, to leave behind everything in which we take pleasure – our homeland, our kindred. Even Jesus spoke of leaving father and mother to follow him. We receive no grace unless we are likewise obedient and journey to the high country to worship God, Cyril suggests. He ranges around the details of the story, but the same basic idea keeps recurring. Abraham's journey shows the importance of changing whole-heartedly, of loving the desert – in other words, loving the purity of heart and mind that humanity enjoyed in the beginning.

So Cyril reaches the story of the Exodus, another exemplar of the same fundamental truth. Both descents into Egypt are seen as the result of free choice, but the consequence is enslavement and oppression. Pharaoh in each case stands for the devil. Human souls are oppressed and put to hard and useless labour, as the Israelites were. For the Israelites God appointed Moses. Now he writes the Law on the heart through Christ, the Mediator who brings us life.

Our second example, the Syrian poet Ephrem, sees the same universal story played out time and again in scriptural narratives. The thirteenth of his *Hymns on Paradise* is a case in point: the King of Babylon resembles Adam; in King David God depicts Adam:

> Because it was not easy for us to see our fallen state –
> How and whence we had fallen at the very outset –
> He depicted it all together in that king,
> Portraying our fall in his fall,
> And portraying our return in his repentant return.[31]

Further verses display Samson, Jonah and Joseph in the same light; they all become examples of this pattern of being cast out and rescued. So again the overarching story of the Bible as understood in the Christian reading, a story of Fall and Redemption, is found in one biblical narrative after another. And journeying through the wilderness is a motif that can sum up the whole saga.

2. Towards appropriation

So far we have been observing how this kind of typology, or figural reading, worked in the life and spirituality of the early

Church. I do not propose that we simply follow them uncritically, but I do want to urge a creative appropriation of this approach. It is not, I suggest, all that different from what happens when we read novels or go to the theatre. Empathy means we come away with our consciousness in some sense transformed. The story and the characters come alive in our imagination as we make an emotional identification with them, and, as Aristotle put it, we experience pity and fear. He suggested that this effects 'katharsis'. The famous director, Peter Brook,[32] warned against interpreting this as 'an emotional steam-bath'. I think it is important to remember that katharsis is a religious word – it means 'purification'. Elsewhere[33] I have explored the idea that theatre, especially tragic drama, is, like sacrifice,[34] a way of facing up to the horrific realities of human nature, both collective and individual – putting violence, death and bloody horror into a ritual context, turning it into a means of purification and atonement, so transforming it into something life-giving. Michael Tippett's work, *A Child of Our Time*, exemplifies the corporate dimensions of this possibility. Mary Douglas[35] suggested a parable which brings out this point: the gardener removes the weeds, so as to 'purify' the flowerbeds; then he puts the weeds in the compost bin, and later restores them to the garden, since they have become life-giving. Through Lent and Holy Week we liturgically live that katharsis, and what the Fathers suggest is that through a similar engagement with the narratives and characters of the Bible, we can discover what our lives are all about.

All this might suggest that this is not a very startling recovery: don't we do it already? 'Life is a journey' is surely a cliché, as is the phrase, 'wilderness experience'. But I think there are two good reasons for suggesting that these clichés need re-minting, and that what we have observed could impinge more effectively on where we are.

The first reason arises from current ways in which people read the Bible, or use it as a weapon. Many are afraid to treat it like a novel or drama because of the battles about its truth that have raged since the nineteenth century. The fundamentalist reader and the modern biblical scholar using historico-critical methods are the obverse and reverse of the same coin. They are concerned with the Bible as fact, as real history; so the focus is on the truth behind the text, the exact reference of the words and narratives. Compared with early Christian interpretation, this is earthbound, literalising – a physical or material approach. The patristic authors consistently show how the words point beyond themselves, how the Bible is really about transformation, about change, about the conversion of the reader. It is not the material or physical that matters but the spiritual. Difficulties in the text, inconsistencies or impossibilities, the *aporiai* (to use the ancient Greek word redeployed by the post-modern intellectual, Derrida) were put there specially to provoke the reader into seeking deeper insight, into searching for the *skopos* or intent of the Holy Spirit.[36] They were able to develop a creative use of the Bible, rather than a defensive or aggressively dogmatic use, because they began with the idea that the Bible points beyond itself. They knew you needed inspiration to interpret the sacred text, and so to develop it in homiletic, pastoral, evocative and imaginative ways. There has to be interaction between text and reader; there are multiple potential meanings, because the Bible speaks in many different ways, many different languages, to people in many different places, cultures, situations, or dilemmas.[37]

Secondly, and more particularly concerning the 'wilderness motif', we should remind ourselves of the post-Enlightenment tendency to view suffering, atrocity, and so on, as grounds for atheism. The current assumptions of our culture include the notion that all ills can be removed, death can be indefinitely postponed and all risk can be eliminated, if we can only find the right formula. This has been reinforced by the success of modern medicine, and the assumption that we all have the right to treatments that will cure whatever afflicts us. The media encourage us in our refusal to face our vulnerability, mortality and creatureliness. The presupposition is that bad things shouldn't happen, or certainly shouldn't happen to good people; and since they do happen and the world is imperfect, there cannot be a God. Indeed, the world is so dreadful, as it impinges on us in our living-rooms on the small screen, that trying to put it right or make sense of it seems beyond us – as compassion fatigue sets in, and we find ourselves lost and insecure, confronted with a world so threatening that the most noticeable reaction is the creation of comfort zones. Indeed, religion itself is reduced to a private comfort zone, which the majority rejects as 'pie in the sky when you die', while those of us who hang on in there are the more anguished about the state of the world, or the awful things that happen to us or those we know, and the insistent doubts and questions which are raised. We all want utopia now and cannot understand why things are the way they are. The clichés, 'life is a journey' or 'going through a wilderness experience', have lost their power to shape the way we handle life.

Or have they?

Some time ago a friend recommended a book to me; it is called *The Solace of Fierce Landscapes*, written by someone called Belden Lane. In many ways it is the book I have dreamed of writing – well, maybe not quite! I wouldn't and couldn't have done it his way, for it is a very personal exploration in which three things are brought together: firstly, the kind of desert history and spirituality I have been sharing here; secondly, his own experiences of journeying in wilderness places, both in the American West and Mount Sinai; and thirdly, his journey alongside his dying mother, through the crisis of cancer and the long wilderness of Alzheimer's. In other words, he explores the inner and outer wildernesses and their relationship. To quote Philip Sheldrake from the dust cover:

> Belden Lane has written a rich, complex and courageous book ... [He] explores how the themes of desert and mountain landscapes are used as metaphors within the Christian spiritual traditions for a painful and purging solitude that paradoxically

offers liberation and inner healing. Underlying his profound exposition of the tradition, however, is another exploration – of his own experiences of grief, pain and struggle ...

It is in this correlation of the physical reality of wilderness and the spiritual, metaphorical, biblical motif that the book rings so many bells for me, out of a different yet parallel journey:

1. There's the 'me' who is theologian and academic, exploring the Bible and the early Church and the wilderness typology in the Christian tradition.

2. There's me, the lover of mountains and wilderness, who nearly 40 years ago had a brush with death on a 20,000-foot peak in the Peruvian Andes, and who, as recently as 2003 and despite increasing age, reached 3000 metres in the French Alps, partly on foot, mostly on a bicycle – the person who relishes challenge, journeying in faith, being overwhelmed by the experience of exposure on cliff-tops and the awe that comes from a sense of smallness in a vast, indifferent world.

3. There's me, the mother of Arthur. Born with profound learning disabilities, he is almost 40 as I write, with extreme physical disabilities arising from his failure to progress as a child. He is totally dependent for all his everyday functions, such as feeding, washing, dressing, mobility – another kind of emptiness, poverty, mystery ...

Some years ago I was at a gathering of theologians at the original L'Arche community in Trosly-Breuil, France. A Lebanese priest gave a little paper in which he drew some interesting parallels between the experience of monks in the wilderness of Syria and the experience of those who choose to live in L'Arche communities. For me it was the most memorable moment of that meeting, and I was pleased to be able to translate the paper for inclusion in the book that emerged from several such meetings.[38] Reflecting on the desert ascetics, Father Youakim Moubarac was searching for parallel experiences in the modern world: he spoke of hospitalisation, imprisonment and confinement in concentration camps, and then suggested that

L'Arche goes further, particularly in producing a radical resolution of the tension between the active life and the contemplative life. I quote:

> In as far as I understand Jean Vanier, daily dealings with people who have handicaps makes those involved face their own violence. Confronted by the irreducibility of the other, the one whom they mean to serve but whose condition they cannot ameliorate, they discover with horror that they are capable of striking them, or even wanting to do away with them. It is this, then, that I call a privileged desert place. The ancient anchorites took themselves off to the desert, they said, to fight with Satan on his own territory. We know now that it is enough to pay attention to the most defenceless people among us to find ourselves given up to our interior demons. But if only we force ourselves not to lose heart, if only grace comes to the aid of our weakness, we apprehend that to spend time with the poorest of all is not to do them charity, but to allow ourselves to be transformed by them and to apprehend God as gentleness.

This rang true to my own experience – to the fact that there have been moments when I could understand those who bash their babies, when I have had to face those inner demons of self-deception, self-hatred, fear, insecurity, failure, self-concern and even potential violence.

Indeed, my pilgrimage with Arthur has been a kind of Exodus, through the wilderness to the Promised Land. For years I found holding onto faith profoundly difficult. God seemed absent. But then one day, as I got up from a chair to go and do some household chore, I suddenly heard a voice, as it were: 'It makes no difference to me whether you believe in me or not!' It was meaningful at all kinds of levels: for one thing, I was absolved of responsibility for deciding about God, for God no longer depended on me for existence – God just 'is', independent of what I thought or felt. Later I discovered that Thomas Merton had been converted, when studying medieval philosophy, by discovering the concept of God's aseity: that is, the reality that God just is, *a se* ('of himself').[39] The need to let go of pre-occupations and anxieties, to journey into the unknown, to accept the utter transcendence and incomprehensibility of God, allowed me a renewal of faith, and soon afterwards a sense of vocation in which Arthur became a central part of my ministry. Overall, my journey has involved a profound shifting away from the questions of theodicy, from the anguished questioning of a Job, to a sense that through the wilderness of coping with Arthur I have had privileged access to a deeper sense of meaning and value – indeed, the deepest truths of Christian theology. It is in the desert that you grow, pruned and purged so that the fruits of the Spirit can germinate when the rains come.

So far my three desert motifs parallel those of Belden Lane fairly closely, but I also want to go further and outline a fourth:

4. There's the 'me' who has been privileged to be in personal touch with many of the issues of our (post-)modern world, the world of violence and struggle. Let me mention a few examples:

(a) Revd Theo Kotze had led the Christian Institute in Cape Town during the struggle against Apartheid. He was a banned person who escaped into exile, settled in Birmingham and became a friend. I shall never forget the first time I met him and heard him preach: he told the story of his undercover journey to Botswana, and then read Psalm 27 – it was as though he had written it himself! Scripture gave him words in which to express himself.

(b) The Conference of European Churches invited me to Belgrade in 1995, after Bosnia and before Kosovo, for a conference with the Serbian Orthodox Church on reconciliation. Another invitee was someone from Northern Ireland. We sat side by side on a bus one day, and he told me how much his generation honoured the memory of the pioneers for peace in Northern Ireland, including my father, who had lived and worked there for some 20 years of the Troubles, and had been a great ecumenist and a friend of Cardinal Cahal Daly.

(c) When Saddam Hussein's statue was felled to the ground, I

Brokenness and Blessing

was in Doha, one of a team of Christian scholars meeting Muslim scholars under the chairmanship of the Archbishop of Canterbury, at the invitation of the Emir of Qatar. In small groups we studied the Bible and the Qur'an side by side, discovering many of the same hermeneutical issues, learning to respect the integrity of those with whom we met. Meanwhile the world's media pressed us for a statement on immediate events ...

These experiences give me a sense that the global and individual dimensions of human life are not separate, but mirrored in one another. The universal and the particular belong together. I remember going to the maternity clinic, and suddenly realising that this most personal and privately meaningful event of being pregnant with a child was happening to so many other people – a common or universal human passage. So it is possible for the depths of private anguish to be taken up into prayerful anguish for the whole human condition. Solitary, contemplative prayer becomes a commitment to compassion and a contribution to the salvation and healing of the whole human race.

It is a paradox that so often God is met *in extremis*. The diaries of Etty Hillesum, recently published in their entirety, are a quite remarkable testimony to that reality. On 2 September 1943 she wrote:

> Now we've grown a little older ... we have become marked by suffering for a whole lifetime. And yet life in its unfathomable depths is so wonderfully good ... If we care just enough, God is in safe hands with us, despite everything ...

Five days later, on 7 September, she was on a transport to Auschwitz, determined to share her people's fate. In a letter to a friend in mid August she had written:

> I am not challenging You, O God; my life is one great dialogue with You. I may never become the great artist I would really like to be, but I am already secure in You, God. Sometimes I try my hand at turning out small profundities and uncertain short stories, but I always end up with just one single word:

God. And that says everything, and there is no need for anything more. And all my creative powers are translated into
inner dialogues with You. The beat of my heart has grown
deeper, more active, and yet more peaceful, and it is as if I were
all the time storing up inner riches.

We live in a world of violence and conflict and pray for peace.
We deplore suffering, injustice and poverty, but live comfortably
off the oppression of others. We worry about where God is when
faced with genocide or our own vulnerability and mortality, and
the majority of our contemporaries have decided there cannot be
a God, given the state of the world. It is this whole complex
context which demands that we move beyond an easy spirituality
of personal well-being, comfort and happiness to rediscover the
wilderness way that lies at the heart of the Bible. It is not easy and
the challenges are profound. It demands a loss of security and
maybe a re-configuring of the God who meets us – we will see in
the next stage of our journey. What we have discovered so far is
that using the Bible figuratively provides maps and guides for the
journey. It makes it possible for us to make our own the narratives, prophetic challenges, provocative words and poetry of
Scripture. So I end with my own psalm, written as a testimony to
my call to ordination, and indebted to Psalms 30 and 116:[40]

> I will exalt you, O Lord,
>> For you have drawn me up from the depths,
>>> And have not suffered hopelessness to triumph over me.
>
> O Lord my God, I cried out in my emptiness,
>> And you have made me whole.
>
> You brought me back from the wilderness places,
>> You saved my life from among those who know you not.
>
> Sing praises to the Lord, all you his faithful ones,
>> And give thanks to his holy name.
>
> Gracious and righteous is the Lord,
>> Full of compassion is our God.

Brokenness and Blessing

For you, O Lord, delivered my soul from the shadow,
　My eyes from tears and my feet from falling.

So I will walk before the Lord
　In the land of the faithful.

I believed I was lost,
　I was brought very low,
　　I said in my haste: 'There is no God.'

The Lord tested me,
　He tested my mind,
　　He tested my heart.

When I was a student, I thought I should be a minister,
　But I was a woman, and the door was then shut.

Nonetheless I went on to study the Scriptures,
　To seek knowledge of the things of God,
　　Convinced I had to, in spite of the barriers.

But the Lord drove me into the wilderness
　And hid his face from me.

Vainly I cried out, 'What is your will, O God?'

The Lord afflicted me,
　He made me taste the waters of bitterness, creation's sadness:
　　My first-born was severely disabled.

Vainly I cried out, 'Why, O God, have you deserted us?'

The Lord showed me all the wickedness of the heart,
　All the injustice in the world,
　　All the warfare of humanity.

Vainly I cried out, 'Where, O God, shall we find you?'

In despair I said,
　'Either God is a demon,
　　Or there is no God.'

But the Lord took pity on me,
   He heard my cry.

In the inner depths of my mind,
   I heard a voice:

'I am the Lord,
   Believe in me or not –
      It makes no difference to *me*.'

Then I knew it was the Lord,
   And my heart was humbled.

As I journeyed on my way,
   Again he spoke to me:

'Go, teach and preach,
   Be my minister.

For this I prepared you from birth,
   For this I led you through the wilderness,
      For this I am setting you on your feet
         And putting my joy and love within your heart.'

Then my heart leapt within me,
   And my being was filled with song:

O give thanks to the Lord, for he is good,
   For his mercy endures for ever.

But who am I that I should serve him thus?
   The tempter spoke of pride.
      The call of the Lord I hid within myself.

But in due time the Lord opened the doors,
   And gave me the conviction to press on along the way.

He made the teacher a preacher,
   He made the lost sheep a shepherd,
He nurtured things in me I'd never known were there.

He put words in my mouth
  And prayers on my lips
    And love in my heart.

He shaped my ministry,
  He took up into my ministry the whole of my past,
    My studies and my sufferings – even my disabled son.

So the questionings of my heart were stilled,
  The doubts of my mind were silenced.

The Lord has shown me what is his will
  And so I declare it to you.

How then shall I repay the Lord for all his benefits to me?

I shall take the cup of salvation
  And call upon the name of the Lord.

O Lord, I am your servant,
  Your servant and the descendant of your servants;
    You have unloosed my bonds.

I will offer you a sacrifice of thanksgiving,
  And call upon the name of the Lord.

I will pay my vows to the Lord
  In the presence of all his people,
In the courts of the house of the Lord,
  Even in the midst of the congregation.

Praise the Lord with me.

Chapter 2
∞∞∞∞∞∞∞∞∞∞∞∞∞∞∞∞∞

WRESTLING JACOB

Come, O thou Traveller unknown,
Whom still I hold, but cannot see!
My company before is gone,
And I am left alone with thee;
With thee all night I mean to stay,
And wrestle till the break of day.

In vain thou strugglest to get free;
I never will unloose my hold!
Art thou the Man that died for
　me?
The secret of thy love unfold:
Wrestling, I will not let thee go,
Till I thy name, thy nature know.

What though my shrinking flesh
　complain,
And murmur to contend so long?
I rise superior to my pain,
When I am weak, then I am
　strong;
And when my all of strength shall
　fail,
I shall with the God-Man prevail.

I need not tell thee who I am,
My misery and sin declare;
Thyself hast called me by
　myname;
Look on thy hands, and read it
　there:
But who, I ask thee, who art thou?
Tell me thy name, and tell me
　now.

Wilt thou not yet to me reveal
Thy new, unutterable name?
Tell me, I still beseech thee, tell;
To know it now resolved I am:
Wrestling, I will not let thee go,
Till I thy name, thy nature know.

Yield to me now; for I am weak,
But confident in self-despair;
Speak to my heart, in blessings
　speak,
Be conquered by my instant
　prayer;
Speak, or thou never hence shalt
　move,
And tell me if thy name is Love.

'Tis Love! 'Tis Love! Thou diedst for me!
I hear the whisper in my heart;
The morning breaks, the shadows flee,
Pure, universal love thou art;
To me, to all, thy mercies move:
Thy nature and thy name is Love.

I know thee, Saviour, who thou art,
Jesus, the feeble sinner's friend;
Nor wilt thou with the night depart,
But stay and love me to the end;
Thy mercies never shall remove:
Thy nature and thy name is Love.

Contented now upon my thigh
I halt, till life's short journey end;
All helplessness, all weakness, I
On thee alone for strength depend;
Nor have I power from thee to move:
Thy nature and thy name is Love.

My prayer has power with God; the grace
Unspeakable I now receive;
Through faith I see thee face to face,
I see thee face to face, and live!
In vain I have not wept and strove:
Thy nature and thy name is Love.

The Sun of Righteousness on me
Has risen with healing in his wings;
Withered my nature's strength, from thee
My soul its life and succour brings;
My help is all laid up above:
Thy nature and thy name is Love.

Lame as I am, I take the prey,
Hell, earth and sin with ease o'ercome;
I leap for joy, pursue my way,
And as a bounding hart fly home,
Through all eternity to prove
Thy nature and thy name is Love.

Charles Wesley's extraordinary poem, occasionally sung as a hymn, is based on the story in Genesis 32:26–32. Jacob is returning to meet Esau. Given the deceit whereby he had obtained the inheritance, he is, not unnaturally, worried about possible revenge. He sends in advance generous gifts as a sign of peace, makes preparations for the fateful meeting, and then waits alone at the brook Jabbok. A man wrestles with him, but cannot prevail against Jacob. He strikes Jacob's hip, however, and Jacob is disabled. Jacob will not let go of his assailant without a blessing. The stranger wants to know who Jacob is, and implicitly in the act of revealing his identity, Jacob admits he is a cheat. He is given a new name, 'Israel'. Jacob now wants to know the name of his contender, but the question is not answered, though the blessing is given. Jacob then calls this place 'Peniel', because he has seen God here and lived. It was, of course, stated elsewhere in Scripture that no one may see God and live (e.g. Exod. 33:20). Finally Jacob limps off, and soon Esau runs to meet him, embraces and kisses him, and they weep together.

This is a mighty intriguing story, to which modern exegetes have given a range of explanations. It probably derives from very ancient oral sagas and has already received layers of interpretation before being incorporated into the biblical story of Israel's ancestor. One commentator asserts: 'It is not God but a hostile demon that attacks the traveller, and this does not in any way change right to the end of the narrative.'[1] There is an animist notion in the background, he suggests, whereby if one knows the name of the spirit, one has power over it. Elsewhere in his discussion he identifies the stranger as 'the river demon who wanted to stop him crossing', describing it as powerful at night but losing strength at daybreak – a common folkloric motif. Another commentator[2] lists the layers that can be identified in the story: in addition to the notion of a 'river spirit who has to be placated or defeated before the traveller can cross', and 'the belief that spirits or ghosts who haunt the night are doomed to disappear before daybreak', he notes that the story provides explanations of (1) the name of the brook – Jabbok is related to the Hebrew for 'wrestling'; (2) the name 'Israel', which means 'the one who strives with God'; (3) the place-name, Peniel, which means 'face of God', and was, possibly, a sanctuary where worship involved a limping ritual dance; and (4) the origin of a food-taboo – for the story ends with a statement whereby it justifies the Israelite refusal to eat the thigh muscle of the hip-socket, because that was where Jacob was struck.

Be all that as it may, most commentators recognise that now, placed here in the text of Genesis, the story legitimises Jacob's stolen blessing and prepares the way for reconciliation with Esau. It seems that what may once have been a midnight struggle with a demon or angel (cf. Hos. 12:3–4), in which the hero with superhuman strength almost overcomes the mysterious super-natural being so as to extort divine power for his own benefit (another common folklore motif), has here become the story of Jacob's surrender of his name and identity to the God who becomes known as the God of Israel. Placed in a great 'aetio-logical' narrative about Israel's origins, it implicitly provides a 'type', summing up Israel's history with God.[3] Robert Davidson comments: 'The history of the people of Israel was often to be a tale of just such an encounter with God; a costly turbulent struggle in the darkness of tragedy, exile and persecution, but an authentic experience in which they came face to face with God.'[4]

For Charles Wesley, however, the 'type' is related to his own soul, and the story of its salvation. He is left alone to wrestle (v. 1), demanding to know who is the stranger with whom he struggles (vv. 2–4). Like Jacob, he knows himself a sinner (v. 2) and wrestles for release, wanting to know the name and nature of God in Christ. To see God face to face is to receive God's grace, to know that God is love (vv. 5–8). The soul limps on life's journey as a result (v. 9), and yet is empowered, because it is dependent on God alone (vv. 9–10). Wesley has made the story his own and discovered there the evangelical message. He was apparently anticipated by Luther:

> And so we have this noble chapter, in which you see the marvellous dealing of God with his saints for our comfort and example, so that we may daily ask ourselves if he is also at work with us and be prepared for it.[5]

This intriguing contrast between pre-modern and historico-critical readings of this text provokes the question:

1. What did the Fathers make of this strange story?

The earliest and most common use of this tale is to list it as one of the Old Testament 'theophanies' – that is, stories of God's appearance in human form – stories which the early Church consistently interpreted as revelations of the pre-existent Christ. A whole series were traditionally identified, the most well known being the story of Abraham entertaining angels unawares, a correlation depicted in the famous Trinity ikon of the Lord appearing to Abraham by the oaks of Mamre as three men ate with him (Gen. 18). Referring to this example, Eusebius of Caesarea then continues:

> To Him [Christ], too, when He later appeared to Jacob in a man's shape, Holy Scripture again refers as God – when he said to Jacob: 'No longer shall your name be called Jacob, But Israel shall be your name; for you have prevailed with God.' Then too: 'Jacob called the name of that place The Form of God,' saying: 'For I saw God face to face, and my life was spared.'[6]

This is the line taken over and over again. Already in the second century, Justin[7] speaks of the angel who appears to Jacob as Christ, listing this story with many others from the Jewish Scriptures where the Lord appears. Cyril of Jerusalem,[8] Hilary of Poitiers,[9] Leo the Great[10] and the *Apostolic Constitutions*[11] follow suit in the fourth and fifth centuries. It was a classic *topos* for proving the pre-existence of the Son of God.

The story was thus known and used by many writers in many different contexts. In the majority of references, however, there is no emphasis on the wrestling, only on the theophany. Some, however, did enquire about the wrestling, and that tends to shift the focus into what might be called 'exemplary reading'. Clement of Alexandria draws on this story in his work called *Paedagogus*.[12] A *paedagogus* was a slave who had the task of accompanying a child to school, overseeing his studies and generally making sure he did the equivalent of homework – in other words, he had a function something like that of an instructor or trainer. Clement's book describes how the Logos (Word) is the 'pedagogue' who trains us for salvation. So in this story God appears as Jacob's instructor or trainer, wrestles with him and anoints him against evil. The face of God that he saw was the Logos or Word by whom God is manifested – that is, the pre-existent Word which would be incarnate in Jesus. The Word acts as a trainer for the athlete of God, giving him practice for contending against the powers of evil.

Clement's successor, Origen, gives it a slightly different twist:[13] human nature is limited and powerless in the struggle against evil powers, so the angel wrestled with Jacob, not in the sense of *against* him, but rather *alongside* him. The angel is there to help Jacob in the struggle against evil, wrestling against the principalities and powers that Paul says we have to contend with. This is a spiritual fight, wrestling to endure sufferings, to avoid being provoked into fierce anger, excessive sorrow, the depths of despair or complaint against God. And all this leads Origen into a discussion of the story of Job. So the wrestling became a 'type' of human spiritual struggles, through which we receive God's blessing.

Another twist is given to this by Eusebius in his great work, *The Preparation for the Gospel*. He summarises his approach like this:

> Israel had formerly borne the name of 'Jacob', but instead of 'Jacob' God bestows upon him the name 'Israel', transforming the active and practical man into the contemplative.[14]

This idea depends upon etymological interpretation of the two names, and is developed at greater length elsewhere: Israel has a double name, because he was called Jacob when 'exercised ... in practical habits and modes of life, and experiencing troubles on behalf of religion', the name meaning 'a man in training, an athlete';

> but when afterwards he receives the rewards of victory over his opponents ... and is already in the enjoyment of the blessings of contemplation, then his name also is changed by the God who communes with him, who both vouchsafes to him a vision of God, and bestows by his new name the rewards of diviner gifts and honours ... Israel indicates 'the man who beholds and contemplates': since the very name when translated means 'a man beholding God.'

It is perhaps worth noting that Eusebius' etymologies are not identical with those of modern commentators, and this is one factor that contributes to very different approaches.

Hilary of Poitiers[15] makes Jacob an example to us to help us in the struggle against the poisonous hissings of the serpent of unbelief. Jacob prevails in wrestling with one who seems a human being, but he eventually perceives it is God and receives God's blessing, and with this vision of faith becomes Israel. Hilary hastens to explain that the weakness and humanity of the supposed man with whom he struggled is no bar to his being God. This is a 'type' anticipating truths taught by the apostles. He turns to the story of Jacob's ladder, identifying the ladder as Christ, following the Gospel of John in this respect. The incarnation is what gives sense to these stories, and Jacob becomes the type of a believer who responds to this human revelation of God.

The moral struggle tends to dominate interpretation, however. Jerome sees Jacob as strengthened by God in his struggle for virtue,[16] and the limp signifies that after this struggle with God his thigh shrank, he had no children and achieved chastity[17] – a clear example of the then common practice of twisting texts to justify the prevailing ascetic ideology.[18] Augustine, on the other hand, at least in one of his many treatments of this story, thinks the wrestling is to hold onto Christ, which means the struggle to love one's enemy – for if you love your enemy, you do indeed hold Christ.[19]

The exegetical points reviewed so far largely come from incidental comments in all kinds of contexts, not from commentaries on Genesis as such, most of which are extant only in fragments or concentrate on the opening of the book concerning creation. There is one extended treatment, however, and that comes from John Chrysostom's *Homilies on Genesis*, a running series that follows the text of Genesis right through. Here, alone in the patristic material that has been traced, the story is related to the context, namely the whole issue of Jacob's reconciliation with Esau. The incident is a demonstration of God's *philanthropia* or love for humanity; for it shows how God allowed Jacob to wrestle with what is right in the form of a man, so that he would learn not to go to that fateful meeting with bad feelings. Jacob must choose fearfulness, and not meet his brother in a spirit of contest. The man tries to leave because he recognises Jacob's righteousness, but Jacob demands a blessing. Furthermore, the story demonstrates Jacob's faith in asking to know who his assailant is. Thus Chrysostom works through the story line by line, often by implication drawing out morals applicable to the Christian pilgrimage of faith. The climax of the homily is a celebration of reconciliation and of God's love in the incarnation, of which this story provides a 'type'. It is a typical example of how the Fathers found homiletic models through their exegesis of Scripture.

So far, then, we have found theophanic and exemplary readings of the story. We can also trace 'dispensational' readings. In a pair of sermons on Jacob,[20] Augustine identifies Esau with the Jews and Jacob/Israel with the Church. He dwells on the fact that the younger supersedes the elder: the law was given to the Jews, but the law promises the kingdom, and so the blessing is taken from Esau and given to Jacob. Esau's hairiness is a sign of his sins; but the hair on Jacob's shoulders belongs to another – so the Church, like Christ, bears the sins of others. This general perspective is reinforced by the interpretation of many details in the story. 'Behold, it is morning, let me go' is expounded by reference to the risen Christ telling Mary not to touch him, and Paul's statement about no longer knowing Christ according to the flesh: so the Church finds spiritual illumination, the light of truth and wisdom, by contrast with the darkness of night and carnality. But then we find a surprising twist, and a reminder that Augustine was speaking in the context of deep controversies within the Church: Jacob, who represents the Church, is not just blessed but limps. There are Christians who live badly, and the touch of the Lord's hand strikes, as well as giving life. Wheat and tares grow together until the final judgement.

By contrast, in *The City of God*, the limp, and its outworking in the food-taboo, justified associating Jacob, not with the

Church, but with the Jewish people, disabled by their failure to accept the Christ. Here, when Augustine[21] speaks of Jacob as blessed and lame, he suggests that he is blessed in those descendants who believe in Christ, but crippled in respect of those who do not believe. He quotes from the Psalms: 'they limped away from their paths' (LXX Psalm 18:45), referring it to the majority of Jews. Christians thus become the true descendants of Israel – that is, the one who saw the face of God in human form.

The predominant 'theophanic' reading, then, is often found intertwined with 'exemplary' and 'dispensational' readings, and in fact more elaborate Christological readings were generated as time went on. Ambrose, in a sermon which traces the lessons to be learned from Jacob's life,[22] begins with 'exemplary' reading, but soon moves on. First of all, then, Jacob is a model, both of wisdom, in that he saw God face to face and won a blessing, and also of fortitude in striving with God.[23] Ambrose suggests that 'to wrestle with God is to enter on the struggle for virtue, to contend with one who is stronger and to become a better imitator of God than others are'. But then it was 'because Jacob's faith and devotion were unconquerable' that

> the Lord revealed his hidden mysteries to him by touching the side of his thigh. For it was by descent from him that the Lord Jesus was to be born of a virgin, and Jesus would be neither unlike nor unequal to God. The numbness in the side of Jacob's thigh foreshadowed the cross of Christ who would bring salvation to all men by spreading the forgiveness of sins throughout the whole world and would give resurrection to the departed by the numbness ... of his own body.

The sun rising on 'holy Jacob' signifies 'the saving cross of the Lord [which] shone brightly on his lineage'; while 'the Sun of Justice rises on the man who recognises God, because He is Himself the Everlasting Light.'

Generally speaking, then, Jacob is an exemplar for the believer and the stranger is the 'type' of Christ; but Ambrose also has begun to take another approach entirely – both here and

Brokenness and Blessing

elsewhere,[24] he suggests we should imitate the type of Christ in Jacob, linking the paralysing of the thigh with the passion, the cross which achieved the future fellowship of human beings with the angels, of which the ladder at Bethel was a sign. Heaven is open to virtue, so we should follow the patriarchs, he concludes.

Augustine provides another way of linking the story with the passion:[25] the fact that Jacob prevailed over the angel represents the passion of Christ, depicting Christ as the 'willing loser', who though he allows himself to be overcome and crucified, is yet the victor over the powers of evil. This comment is intertwined among the usual points, giving them another dimension: Jacob receives blessing from the angel he defeated, implying that Christ blesses the human race which slew him; and, as the name he is given means 'seeing God', so he receives in anticipation the vision of God which is the reward for the saints at the end of the world.

This exploration of how the Fathers treated one particular enigmatic story has demonstrated how it was possible to play with the text, find multiple meanings through inspired insight, and read one story in terms of another; but it also gives rise to the question whether all interpretations are valid, and how we might establish criteria for deciding what might or might not be appropriate. One criterion which seems vital for Christian interpretation is the context and form of the story as it appears in the canon. The origins of the story may be illuminated by talk of a fight with a river demon, but that idea was re-minted as the story was incorporated first into the J-source, then the book of Genesis, then the Torah, then 'the Law and Prophets', then the Christian Bible. The words of the text point to various possible interpretations, but at the core is the idea of Jacob wrestling with God, a mysterious Being discerned in human form, and being given a new name through the contest. It is this which is captured in our final example, from Gregory Nazianzen.

The theme of Gregory's *Second Theological Oration* is the transcendence of God, the God who is beyond our comprehension. During the discussion he mentions glimmerings of this in Scripture, including Jacob wrestling with God in human form. Gregory is not at all clear what this wrestling means, but he notes that Jacob bore on his body the marks of the wrestling, and this signifies the defeat of the created nature. Gregory acknowledges Jacob's reward in the name-change to 'Israel', but the climax of what he says is this:

> Neither he, nor any of his descendants in the twelve tribes who made up the children of Israel, could boast that he comprehended the whole nature or the pure sight of God.

For Gregory the story is about the human struggle to know God, and its ultimate failure. It is only because God accommodates the divine self to our human level, through the inevitably limited human language of Scripture, and above all by accepting the constraints of incarnation, that we have any chance of knowing anything about God.

Maybe this will prove to be for us the most insightful treatment of the story we have found among the Fathers. My aim here is not to suggest that we take over the interpretation of the Fathers, but rather explore the freedom with which they approached the text, so as to find patterns and approaches that make sense to us. Charles Wesley was in the patristic tradition when he gave evangelical meaning to this story. What would it mean for us to follow suit?

2. Are there parallels, 'types' or possibilities that enable this story to speak to our condition in the (post-)modern world?

Atheism and modernity's struggle with God

Our condition is profoundly shaped by modernity. Since the Enlightenment, European culture has been struggling with the question of God. Wrestling with God's existence or goodness began in earnest with the Lisbon earthquake of 1755. Suddenly, for thinkers across Europe, it no longer made sense to speak of a created order ruled by a gracious providence when tens of thousands had apparently died senselessly. This could hardly be the best of all possible worlds, as Leibnitz had argued. This event, together with the questions about arbitrary and innocent suffering that it raised, haunted subsequent theology. The dominant question became theodicy. The twentieth century did little to alleviate this. The First World War ended the illusion of heroism, as millions died or were traumatised in the trenches. The dehumanised and industrialised genocide of the Holocaust not only demonstrated 'man's inhumanity to man', but also called into question the idea of the biblical God who protected his Chosen People. The advent of radio and television has revealed the sheer ongoing scale of human suffering and atrocity. A university colleague of Jewish descent once commented to me: 'If I were God, I wouldn't let my children do to each other what we humans do.' God's morality is in question, and the best option after Auschwitz appears to be atheism. Samuel Beckett's play, *Waiting for Godot*, captured the mood: there is no God to intervene and sort things out; God either does not exist or is a demon.[26]

So, over the past three centuries Europeans have wrestled with a God who turned out to be powerless. Like Jacob, they found themselves prevailing, and decided God was dead. And this universal story has been played out in the lives of individuals. People have easily lost their faith, especially in the face of personal tragedy. So now the majority of our contemporaries never seem to know or care about their Christian heritage. God has become a mere exclamation in today's language. For most the wrestling is over, and they are neither lamed nor blessed. Yet for some, including myself, wrestling with God has been a desperate plea for blessing, hanging on in there like Jacob, and getting lamed in the process. The struggle centred on my severely disabled son, but largely because he became the symbol of all the 'gonewrongness' that modernity has identified as a good reason for calling God into question.

My account of patristic interpretation had Gregory as its

climax because he provides the clue to one way in which this story might speak. In the end it is the creature that is disabled, defeated in the attempt to know God. For the whole nature of God is beyond creaturely comprehension. Wrestling with God, we may think we are the masters, only to discover that we are the ones who are marked by the struggle and given a new name. For at the heart of that struggle with God is an experience of loss of security and self-sufficiency, of being put in one's place. In the end it is not that we judge God – rather, God judges us; and that implies a need to reconfigure our notions of God. We imagine we are in control, we make up our minds, we decide whether we are religious or not, we choose whether to seek God or not . . . But the whole point is that we are mere limited creatures, vulnerable, far from in control, certainly not capable of grasping the reality of God.

Thomas Merton[27] speaks of 'the one big concept' which was to revolutionise his whole life – the word *aseitas* (briefly mentioned in the previous chapter):

> In this one word, which can be applied to God alone, and which expresses His most characteristic attribute, I discovered an entirely new concept of God – a concept which showed me at once that the belief of Catholics was by no means the vague and rather superstitious hangover from an unscientific age that I had believed it to be. Here was a notion of God that was at the same time deep, simple and accurate and charged with implications which I could at least dimly estimate. *Aseitas* simply means the power of a being to exist absolutely in virtue of itself, requiring no cause, no other justification for its existence except that its very nature is to exist. There can be only one such Being: that is God. And to say that God exists *a se*, of and by reason of Himself, is merely to say that God is Being Itself. *Ego sum qui sum.*

'I am what I am.' I have already mentioned[28] my own experience of wrestling and doubting over many years, which was stopped short by those words: 'It makes no difference to me whether you believe in me or not.' If God just is, that must be true, and it puts me in my place. Pondering the book of Job, that intense debate about God's goodness within the Bible, I began to discern that the answer to Job's questioning was simply the fact that he found himself in God's presence. In God's presence all the questions just fade away, as you realise the immensity of the infinite, divine reality with which you are confronted.

Western Christian theology is often described in terms of 'theism', and theism seems to describe Superman projected onto the heavens, a gigantic monarch, omnipotent, omniscient, and male, of course – a being logically demolished with ease and so conducive to atheism.[29] Eastern Christian theology, the theology of the Greek Fathers and the Orthodox Liturgy, remains profoundly aware of the problems of religious language, of the limitations of human language and thought. Of course, I paint with a broad brush, but it seems to me important to explore this 'apophatic' tradition of theology.

Religious language and the 'otherness' of God

Apophaticism emerged from an earlier struggle with the nature of God. For Christianity, in its struggle with idolatry, picked up the critique long since offered by philosophy.

It is hardly an accident, then, that what we know of Xenophanes, a Greek philosopher of the fifth century BCE, is preserved in the works of Clement of Alexandria, a Christian writer of the third century CE who provides us with this quotation:

> Ethiopians make their gods black with turned-up noses. Thracians make them with red hair and blue eyes. Mortals think that gods are born and have their own food, voice and shape; but if oxen or lions had hands and could draw or produce images like men, horses would draw the shapes of the gods like horses, oxen like oxen, and they would produce such bodies as the bodily frame they have themselves.

Xenophanes thus anticipates Feuerbach and the notion that God is simply a human projection. He is reported to have concluded that there must be one god quite unlike mortals in form and thought: eternal, unoriginate (that is, one who never came into being but always was), impassible (that is, not subject to influence, bribery, pain, emotion, change, and suchlike), as one in everything, neither finite nor infinite, neither moved nor at rest, but the greatest and best of all things. In other words, God must defy the categories of human conception.

A pagan philosopher of the Christian era, Maximus of Tyre, wrote this:

> He is the Mind which is Father and Maker of All, whose name Plato cannot tell because he does not know it, whose appearance he cannot describe because he cannot see it, whose size he cannot estimate, since he cannot touch it. The divine is invisible to the eyes, unspeakable with the voice, untouchable with the flesh, unknown to the hearing: only by the most beautiful, most pure, most intellectual aspect of the soul is it seen through its likeness and heard through its kinship, the whole together being present to the whole understanding ... God has no size, no colour, no form, nor any other accident of matter, but he has a beauty quite unlike any other beauty.

It is not surprising that many modern scholars have spoken of early Christianity adopting the God of Greek philosophy.

Yet in fact all this was radicalised in Christian theology by the biblical teaching against idolatry. To quote Isaiah's satire:

> The carpenter stretches a line, he marks it out with a pencil; he fashions it with planes, and marks it with a compass; he shapes it into the figure of a man ... He cuts down cedars ... Half of it he burns in the fire ... he roasts meat ... also he warms himself and says, 'Aha, I'm warm, I have seen the fire!' And the rest of it he makes into his god ... and worships it ...; he prays to it and says, 'Deliver me, for thou art my god!'

Other prophets, such as Amos, insisted that God could not be bribed with sacrifice. Moses was hidden in a cleft while God's glory passed by – he could see only God's back-parts because 'No one can see God and live.' The Jewish fear of blasphemy meant that already by New Testament times, God's name was never pronounced as Scripture was read. God's only name was 'I am that I am', and through the prophet, God had said, 'My thoughts are not your thoughts, nor are my ways your ways' (Isa. 55:8). God was respected as transcendent holiness, as infinite and essentially incomprehensible, on the basis of key biblical texts. Indeed, this was far from being, as some have suggested, the 'acute Hellenisation' of Christianity,[30] undermining the biblical God. It was an agnosticism borne out of the struggle with idolatry and a recognition of the humility required of those who are mere creatures.

This absolutely transcendent God could only be spoken of in negative terms, by what was called 'analysis' – the systematic abstraction of our earthly experience and knowledge, so as to arrive at a concept of what is 'other': invisible, immaterial, incorporeal, impassible, unchangeable, indivisible, indefinable, infinite, incomprehensible, beyond Being, beyond speech, beyond change, beyond movement, beyond corruption, and so on and so on. Think again of Gregory of Nyssa, of the ideas (outlined in the previous chapter) developed in opposition to the heretic who thought he knew everything about God, of that picture of the endless mountain climb, and the vertigo to be experienced when you try to contemplate God. But it was precisely the inadequacy of the human mind for engaging successfully in this struggle for knowledge of God which, for Christian theologians, opened the way for revelation. They affirmed that, while God is in principle infinite and incomprehensible, nevertheless he has chosen to 'accommodate' the divine self to our human level, to speak to us in human language, even to meet us as a human being in Jesus.

So the Fathers explored the theophanies in the Scriptures which they called the Old Testament, appearances of God as an angel or in human form, of which Wrestling Jacob was one, seeing them as hints of the incarnation to come. They debated biblical language: Athanasius and both Gregories asked about the meaning of 'Son of God', insisting that the language cannot be taken too literally, in the sense that it cannot have the physical connotations it always has in human terms; rather, the language has to be elevated or stretched to refer to what is beyond human physical reality. The Syrian poet, Ephrem, spoke of God clothing the divine self in a 'garment of names':

> Let us give thanks to God who clothed Himself in the names of the body's various parts: Scripture refers to his ears to teach us that he listens to us; it speaks of his eyes to show that he sees us ... Blessed is He who has appeared to our human race under so many metaphors.[31]

He tells a parable of someone teaching a parrot to speak – he hides behind a mirror, so that, when the bird turns in the direction of the voice speaking, it finds its own image reflected and imagines it is speaking to another parrot. God did something very like that, bending down in his love and acquiring our habits of speech. He describes three ways of accommodation to our level: the incarnation, the language of Scripture and the creation:

> The Power of the Father, compelled by his love, descended and dwelt in a virgin womb.[32]

> Lord, you bent down and put on humanity's types so that humanity might grow through your self-abasement ...[33]

> He allows himself to be depicted with various likenesses, so that we learn of him according to our ability.[34]

> Lord, your symbols are everywhere ... Blessed is the Hidden One shining out.[35]

> If the bird gathers its wings, thus denying the extended symbol of the Cross, then the air too will deny the bird; the air will not carry the bird unless its wings confess the Cross.[36]

The word of God comes to us in inadequate words and symbols, yet because it is God who communicates, they do provide some glimmer of the truth which is in principle beyond us. That is why Scripture is so fundamentally important.

So a biblical spirituality informed by the Eastern Fathers necessarily fosters humility, *aporia* – that is, the sense of being at a loss, of losing control over language and concept, moving beyond literalism and the idolatries of our mental projections, knowing that to know is not to know, yet being confronted with a reality beyond the compass of our limited minds, being put in our place, having our pride and competence challenged, discovering our creatureliness, and the fact that we cannot know God without being disabled, as Jacob was. Rowan Williams, giving an account of the same spiritual tradition, entitled his book *The Wound of Knowledge*. Gregory Nazianzen suggested that Jacob's limp signifies the defeat of our created nature.

Creature and Creator

The Christian doctrine of 'creation out of nothing' was a development of profound importance. It was not simply inherited from Judaism – Genesis was ambiguous and variously interpreted until well into the Christian era. It was the debate with Greek philosophy and Gnosticism in the second century which established the basis of a doctrine which would deeply affect Christian understanding from the fourth century onwards.[37]

The dominant philosophy of the time arose out of interpretations of Plato, and his dialogue known as the *Timaeus* was at the centre of debate about cosmic origins. Many Platonists thought the world was eternal, and the 'myth' Plato told was simply symbolic of the eternal relationship between the (divine) Mind, the Ideas or Designs with which it worked and the Matter which it shaped. Others took the myth more literally, and certainly a second-century apologist like Justin Martyr, in the same way as the Jewish philosopher Philo before him, made a correlation between Genesis and the *Timaeus* so as to produce an account of the act of creation by God in the beginning. This implied that God (the Demiurge or Creator) produced everything out of pre-existent Matter by imposing Form or Design upon it – or as Genesis put it, there were the chaos-waters, and the earth was without form and void, before the divine Spirit hovered over the waters and by the Word of God an ordered world emerged from the chaos.

Gnostic ideas were rather different. A spiritual world of eternal beings (*aeons*) emanated from the 'Depth' (*Bythos*) – that is, the infinite, ultimate, unknowable divine whatever – to make up the 'fullness' (*pleroma*) of the divine; whereas the material world was the result of a pre-cosmic 'fall', a terrible accident which trapped spiritual sparks in Matter, salvation being escape back to the spiritual world. The Creator (Demiurge) was a fallen being who had been expelled from the spiritual world.

What emerged from these debates is summed up by Tertullian in the early third century: God did not create out of the divine self, otherwise everything is divine; God did not create out of pre-existent Matter, otherwise there are two eternal, divine Beings; so God must have created out of nothing. Already Theophilus had insisted that God demonstrated superiority to all other craftsmen by creating the stuff out of which he made things. So fundamental to the idea of God as Creator was God's 'Otherness'.

The doctrine of 'creation out of nothing' had, and has, profound consequences:

- It meant a great gulf of difference between God and everything created, including spiritual beings like angels. The twentieth-century mystic, Simone Weil, once wrote: 'the act of creation is an act of abandonment'. By this she implied that nothing could exist which is not God unless the infinite God withdraws and makes space for something 'other' to have being. This is an important insight into the depths of what the Fathers were feeling after. It is simply not enough to think of God creating by analogy with an architect or sculptor.

- It meant that everything depends on God for existence, otherwise creatures sink back into the nothingness from which they were created. Created things are vulnerable and mortal; that is their natural state of being.
- It meant that knowledge of God depends on God taking the initiative to reveal the divine self – God's essential Being is so utterly 'other' that we cannot have a glimmering of God unless we are ready to receive what God offers by reaching across the gulf. We are back with the idea of God's aseity, and the defeat of the created nature in its attempts to know God.

The doctrine of 'creation out of nothing' is, as it were, the other side of the coin, and fundamental to the biblical spirituality of the Fathers. This spirituality can never be some kind of self-fulfilment; it must always have receptivity at its heart. Indeed, acceptance of disability is the condition of blessing.

So back to the story of Wrestling Jacob, and to the way in which it is sometimes associated with the story of Job. The Bible encourages us to be honest with our doubts about God, with our anguish about the way the world is and our frustration at God's absence. 'Was Job blaspheming?' a devout student once asked me in class. It was an opportunity to contest the notion that you should suppress questions and doubts in prayer. The Psalms give us words in which to express these feelings, and the Jewish tradition of challenging and complaining against God is surely one that Christians can learn from. Truth, honesty and integrity belong to spirituality, and it is important in the face of modernity to acknowledge the experience of doubt as a reality. The Fathers sometimes saw the 'type' of Christ in Jacob, and the wrestling and wounding as foreshadowing the cross; and maybe we can align with it the agony in the garden and the cry of desolation. Jesus, in his identification with us, was tried and tested in all points as we are, says the Epistle to the Hebrews, and that sense of abandonment by God, as well as the struggle to say, 'Thy will, not mine', speaks to the same desperation as we feel in the face of atrocity and inexplicable destruction.

Apart from the passion of Christ – that extraordinary story of God bridging the gulf and plumbing the depths of all that is gone wrong in humanity – there is no simple theoretical answer to the theodicy questions, just partial palliatives. In the book of Job we see how the presence of God puts everything into a different perspective. Job's complaints and doubts disappear before the reality of God, which is humbling and judging and renewing. At the end of 1 Corinthians 13 Paul says, 'Now I know only in part'; he expects to 'know fully' in the future, but shifts the focus by adding, 'even as I have been fully known'. God's knowledge of us is both wonderful and fearful, according to Psalm 139. In the end we are put in our place. The spiritual struggle is put on a different footing. It is not about us wrestling with God, but about wrestling with ourselves until the created nature is defeated and we are fit to receive God's blessing.

Spiritual growth through being disabled

Ancient society was nearly as besotted with sport as we are, and athletic training for sporting contests of all kinds (*agōnes*) was a natural metaphor for spiritual struggle. Like athletes in the games, the athletes for Christ sought *doxa* (glory), but *doxa* of a different kind, namely, the glory of God. We find this *agōn*-motif already in the New Testament: Hebrews 12:1 speaks of running the race (*agōn*) set before us, with a great crowd of spectators cheering us on; 1 Corinthians 9:24–27 develops the metaphor:

> Do you not know that in a race the runners all compete, but only one receives the prize? Run in such a way that you may win it. Athletes exercise self-control in all things; they do it to receive a perishable wreath, but we an imperishable one. So I do not run aimlessly, nor do I box as though beating the air; but I punish my body and enslave it, so that after proclaiming to others I myself should not be disqualified.

Paul here provides scriptural warrant for the *encrateia* (self-discipline) practised by the early ascetics. A student of mine once commented that the Syrian monks in the desert had an excellent 'keep fit' regime, with their constant prostrations and vegetarian diet! Some kind of spiritual 'stripping-down' is essential for progress and growth to maturity. It is perhaps no accident that physical stripping and spiritual stripping go hand in hand. Standing on the top of Ranrapalca, that 20,000-foot peak in the Peruvian Andes that I mentioned in the last chapter, there was, of course, a sense of achievement after the struggle, but also a sense of awe, an awareness of littleness in a vast landscape, of vulnerability alongside amazement – one was put in one's place!

Which brings us back to the desert again, and its demanding disciplines. 'Who sits in solitude and is quiet has escaped three wars: hearing, speaking, seeing; yet against one thing he continually battles, that is, his own heart.'[38] Such a sentiment is anticipated by James 1:14: each person is tempted when lured and enticed by his own desire. The struggle is internal because the human heart (if we speak at the individual level), or the human race (if we consider the communal dimension), so easily seeks to revert to being in control, putting itself in God's place. So, as Origen suggested, the real battle is with the powers of evil, the inner demons, and the wonder is that God contends with us, as the angel or human form of God wrestled with Jacob, not against him. It is hardly surprising, after all, that Jacob should wrestle with himself before meeting Esau. He had to take responsibility for what he had done. To receive forgiveness is the hardest thing on earth, because it means admitting you were wrong, and to do that you have to step down from the pedestal of self-justification. As Chrysostom hinted, Jacob's self-pride has to be disabled before he can be reconciled with Esau, so that his stolen blessing can become a blessed responsibility as he receives a new name and vocation. So he anticipates the temptations of Jesus, the challenge to which humanity so easily succumbs – to use power and influence for one's own ends, achieving the worldly *doxa* (glory) that comes with power or popularity, rather than worshipping God and willingly accepting God's will and God's call. The spiritual battleground is within each and every one of us; but

Christ got the better of the devil's challenge, wrestling within himself for 40 days, and again in Gethsemane.

The Macarian Homilies are a classic of Christian spirituality.[39] Attributed to the great ascetic, Macarius, but now recognised as most likely coming from a Syrian background, they have influenced Eastern Orthodox monasticism down the centuries. They were rediscovered and translated by German Pietists, and extracts were published in English by John Wesley in his Christian Library. These homilies affirm that biblical characters, such as Joseph, David, Moses, Abraham, Noah, are there as examples 'to show that the power of divine grace is in the human person and the gift of the Holy Spirit which is given to the faithful soul comes with much contention, with much endurance, patience, trials and testings.'[40] Yet heaven is anticipated among those born of God and we should strive that 'the inward self may be partaker of that glory in this present life'[41] and so 'become the pure habitation of the Holy Spirit' and 'attain heights which the soul does not reach all at once, but through many labours and conflicts, with variety of trials and temptations, it receives spiritual growth and improvement, till at last it comes to an entire exemption from its afflictions.'[42]

I could speak very personally about a radical shift in my own life. For long I struggled with the problem of evil and suffering, embodied for me in my disabled son; for how could I go on believing in a good Creator God when a newly created being was so flawed? It was not for me a question of 'Why me?' but 'Why at all?' – the personal and the global, the individual and the universal reflecting one another. The shift was a move beyond all that to discovering that through my son I have been brought to a very different place – for he has been the catalyst for a deeper appreciation of the core elements of the Christian tradition. I stand alongside him as a vulnerable creature, disabled and mortal, knowing my creaturely limitations and my lack of knowledge, especially of God. I know my need of God and my resistance to God's grace, the inner demons like self-pity that so easily take over my interior life. Yet again and again I find myself lamed and blessed. I discern signs of God's presence, I meet God in human form, I discover glimpses of Christ, in the faces of some of the most damaged and disabled human persons. One such occasion was during the Faith and Light pilgrimage to Lourdes in 1991 when the story of Mary Magdalene meeting the Risen Christ, whom she thought was the gardener, was mimed by a woman with profound learning disabilities, and Jesus was played by a man with Down's Syndrome.

So, as for Charles Wesley, then also for me, Wrestling Jacob has become a symbol, a 'type', of the Christian life as I've experienced it, and I too have discovered that the name of the one with whom I struggle is indeed LOVE.

Chapter 3

THE WAY OF JESUS

My song is love unknown,
My Saviour's love to me,
Love to the loveless shown,
That they might lovely be.
  O who am I,
  That for my sake
  My Lord should take
  Frail flesh and die?

He came from his blest throne,
Salvation to bestow;
But men made strange, and none
The longed-for Christ would
    know.
  But O my Friend,
  My Friend indeed,
  Who at my need
  His life did spend!

Sometimes they strew his way,
And his sweet praises sing;
Resounding all the day
Hosannas to their King.
  Then 'Crucify!'
  Is all their breath,
  And for his death
  They thirst and cry.

Why, what hath my Lord done?
What makes this rage and spite?
He made the lame to run,
He gave the blind their sight.
  Sweet injuries!
  Yet they at these
  Themselves displease,
  And 'gainst him rise.

They rise, and needs will have
My dear Lord made away;
A murderer they save,
The Prince of Life they slay.
  Yet cheerful he
  To suffering goes,
  That he his foes
  From thence might free.

In life no house, no home,
My Lord on earth might have;
In death no friendly tomb
But what a stranger gave.
  What may I say?
  Heaven was his home;
  But mine the tomb
  Wherein he lay.

Here might I stay and sing,
No story so divine:
Never was love, dear King,
Never was grief like thine!

This is my Friend,
In whose sweet praise
I all my days
Could gladly spend.

What a contrast with the modern 'Quest for the Historical Jesus'![1] It is not that the hymn lacks certain concrete items of the Jesus story: we recognise the Triumphal Entry to Jerusalem (v. 3), the healing miracles (v. 4), the saying about the Son of Man having nowhere to lay his head (v. 6), and especially the passion-narrative (vv. 3–5); but the hymn is not really interested in what we would call the 'facts' of history or 'authentic' Jesus material. Rather, it focuses on love, on one who is 'my Saviour'. It emphasises the condescension or humiliation of the one who relinquished his higher status freely and willingly, to suffer rejection and homelessness, and to face pain and death; and this emphasis is intended to evoke an appropriate response of love and praise for the grief, the suffering, the death, all borne on behalf of the singer.

The hymn follows a similar pattern to patristic interest in the earthly life of Jesus. It is a pattern based on Philippians 2:5–11 and presupposing the theology of the last chapter – the gulf between God's 'Otherness' and our creatureliness bridged by the saving *kenōsis* (emptying) in the incarnation. It is not a bit like a modern biography, seeking to reconstruct the life of the subject in a standard kind of way: dates, parentage, upbringing, influences, actions and events, teaching (*ipsissima verba*), psychological development, intention and aims, cause of death, nature of opponents, and so on. So did the Fathers have any interest in the historical Jesus? The answer is 'Yes – they did'; but their interest was different, and what makes it different is, I suggest, crucial for the development of a biblical spirituality.

1. The Fathers and the Jesus of history

Anti-docetic interest

By the turn of the first and second centuries, groups of Christians were apparently assuming that the Christ was a supernatural being who did not really get born, suffer and die. It is not entirely clear exactly what they did think. For some,[2] it would seem, the Christ came onto the human Jesus at his baptism and retreated again prior to his crucifixion – in fact they appealed to the Gospels, claiming that Jesus cried out on the cross, 'My power, my power, why hast thou forsaken me?' Others perhaps envisaged a kind of angel dressed up in human guise, such as is found in the book of Tobit.[3] Revelation of spiritual truths seems to have been the focus, and salvation was regarded as escape from material existence. So for these people the earthly, historical life of the Saviour was not relevant – indeed, not real.

To such teaching there was an immediate and strong reaction. Ignatius, bishop of Antioch around 110 CE, wrote letters to the churches of Asia Minor as he was transported to Rome for martyrdom. He asserted[4] that 'he [Christ] was truly born, truly ate and drank, was truly persecuted under Pontius Pilate, truly was crucified and died, and ... truly raised from the dead', against those who claimed that 'he suffered in phantom only', his climax being the affirmation that 'His Father raised him up, who will in like manner raise us up who believe in him – indeed His Father will raise us in Christ Jesus, apart from whom we have not true life.' For Ignatius the eucharistic elements were 'the medicine of immortality'.[5] So we can see that the main motif of the concrete story he defends is the imparting of true life to us through Christ's real sharing in our life and death. No one would bother suffering martyrdom for a phantom, says Ignatius, as he journeys to Rome expecting to be thrown to the wild beasts.[6]

As we move through the second century, we find an increasing correlation between defence of Christ's real human life and defence of the goodness of God's creation. There were huge cultural pressures to idealise the perfect, unchangeable world of the spirit over against the corruptibility and impermanence of the material creation. God belonged to the former and could not be contaminated by the latter. It was such assumptions that encouraged docetism. So even if God were Creator, it was all done at arm's length, so to speak, through mediators, like angels. Some, such as the Gnostics, regarded the material world as the result of an accident or fall in the spiritual realm (or the divine *Plerōma*). Matter, then, was inherently faulty. Hence the attraction of escape through the planetary spheres to the non-material realm from which spiritual beings originated and to which they would return. By the end of the second century Irenaeus was determined to counter such teaching.

For Irenaeus, God was the Creator of the material world and God saw it was good, as the Bible stated in its opening verses. The material world and our bodily existence were therefore to be valued. Matter was not the result of a fall; the real Fall came with Adam's disobedience, not prior to creation. The whole point of the incarnation was that a second Adam went over the ground again, tempted and tried in all points as we are, yet without being disobedient. In fact, Irenaeus' theology is well captured in Newman's hymn, 'Praise to the Holiest in the Height', especially in the phrase, 'a second Adam to the fight and to the rescue came'. This 'recapitulation' of the Adam story[7] required a genuine incarnation, a really authentic, fleshly, human being. Furthermore, for Irenaeus, the Eucharist is our offering of the first-fruits of creation[8] – there is no real Eucharist for those who do not believe in creation's goodness and the reality of Christ's flesh. God's purpose is the restoration of creation to the fullness of God's intention. This is consummated in Christ. The material and the spiritual belong together within God's intentions. The divorce of soul and body denies the reality of our existence. The divorce of Jesus and Christ denies the incarnation. The divorce of God from creation denies God's goodness and providence: Christ and the Spirit are, as it were, the two hands of God,[9] the instruments whereby God engages in creating and restoring the divine work.

So Irenaeus was not primarily interested in the life and teaching of Jesus as history in the modern sense – precisely what happened, which were the authentic sayings, and so on – but he was most certainly determined that it was all real. For the early Fathers, the four Gospels were, though different in detail, records of what had actually happened during the earthly life of Christ – the 'memoirs of the apostles', as Justin put it.[10] At least one gospel circulating at the end of the second century, the *Gospel of Peter*, was rejected because of its docetic features[11] – that is, it did not consistently present the reality of what we would call the historical Jesus. By the fourth century we can discern a very concrete sense of needing to be 'in touch' with this reality: the Empress Helena is said to have prayed on earth where the feet of Jesus had trod,[12] and pilgrimage to the Holy Land began. But above all it was in the Eucharist that Christians felt in touch – the sacrament being the vehicle of the divine life, the extraordinary in the ordinary material of earthly existence.

Apologetic interest

Concern with the truth of the story told in the Gospels also arose from apologetic need, the necessity for Christians to explain themselves to outsiders and justify their claims.

1. The events of Jesus' life established the fulfilment of prophecy. For Justin this was the strongest proof of the truth of Christianity. Jesus was not a magician, he argues,[13] and miracles are (so to speak) two a penny; thus they do not constitute a proof. On the other hand, the fact that everything was predicted in the books of the Hebrew prophets shows that Christian claims are valid. Clearly, the early Christians had a very different mind-set from ours. In the work known as his *First Apology*, Justin tells the life of Jesus, not by recounting the stories found in the Gospels, but by quoting prophecies about his lineage, the manner and place of his birth, his suffering and death, his resurrection and future judgement, the response of the Gentiles, and so on.[14] In his *Dialogue with Trypho*, whether this was a report of a real dialogue

with a Jew or simply a literary device for confirming the argument with prophecy, he sets out to show that Christian interpretation is superior to Jewish because fulfilment can be demonstrated. The laws prefigure Christ and have their 'end' (that is, both their finish and their fulfilment) in him. The prophecies are fulfilled: Justin proceeds to work through all the classic proof-texts, including 'A virgin shall conceive' (Isa. 7:14; quoted by Matt. 1:23) and the verses of Zechariah (9:9; 14:4) associated with the Triumphal Entry (e.g. Matt. 21:1–9), and many others.

2. Justin quotes and affirms much of the teaching to be found in the Gospels in order to show how it goes beyond anything heard before.[15] The kind of teaching Jesus gave demonstrates that he is greater than other philosophers, though Justin admits that God's Word or Wisdom was already partially known by Socrates[16] as by the prophets – for there is one God and all truth comes from him. The superiority of Jesus' ethical teaching is shown in his commands to love your enemies and give to the poor and needy. There are many stories from the early Church about Christians impressing people by their extraordinary behaviour: they despised death, so stayed behind in plague-ridden cities to tend the sick,[17] and martyrs converted the soldiers who imprisoned and tortured them.[18] The teaching and example of Jesus undergirded the claim to a superior ethic.

3. The events of Jesus' life were not to be regarded as mere myth like those of the gods and heroes of Greek tradition. The biggest exposition of this is to be found in Origen's answer to the pagan critic of Christianity, Celsus.[19] He had mocked the idea that a god would need to go to Egypt to escape death from Herod; 'a god wouldn't have a body like yours', he asserted, and 'the body of a god wouldn't need food'. As for suffering, how can you claim a god suffers? The stories are obviously all false, he implies – the resurrection appearances must be hallucinations: he should have appeared to those who condemned him to prove himself right! Or else he should have just disappeared from the cross. Origen has to concede analogies between some of the

Gospel stories and pagan myths (e.g. the so-called 'virgin birth'), but he works hard to claim the reality of Christ's public execution and to explain how these earthly stories point to deeper truths.

Now, modern historical interest has also a strong apologetic motivation. It was the scepticism of the nineteenth century about Church dogma, supernaturalism and miracles that gave rise to the so-called 'Quest for the Historical Jesus'. In a way the Questers also wanted to be in touch with a realistic Jesus, a Jesus who, for them, embodied the highest ideals of the nineteenth-century European outlook. So Jesus became the exponent of the Fatherhood of God and the brotherhood of Man, the supreme religious genius, a great personality who founded a new religion at a turning-point in history. This was, as for the Fathers, an apologetic endeavour, but in a different intellectual environment, faced with different questions and anxieties about the basis of faith. The Quest has continued to be fuelled by the rise of historical consciousness and scientific understanding of the world, and the so-called 'Third Quest', belonging to the decades leading up to the Millennium, has been driven by the need to rediscover a credible Jesus within his own historical context. Of fundamental importance, in the post-Holocaust world, has been a re-emphasis on the fact that Jesus was a Jew.[20] Yet interest in the historical Jesus still tends to be iconoclastic, to seek an elimination of the layers of faith and dogma which affect the story, even in the Gospels. Maybe the important point we could learn from the Fathers is that this material, historical reality of Jesus is fundamentally important, but always because the life and teaching of Jesus points beyond itself. It is not enough to show that Jesus was a sage like other wisdom-teachers or Cynic philosophers; or that he was a seer like other prophets and holy men of his time – to mention but two of the categories used by Third Questers. It is not enough because the earthly, material, historical reality is only part of what it is about. The pattern of Jesus' life fulfilled a kind of destiny, as he willingly and obediently followed the way God set before him, living out what he taught, providing an example, but

Brokenness and Blessing

even more, making it possible for the divine life to be restored to humanity.

Interest arising from the exemplary character of Jesus' life

Early Christianity was principally focused on issues about way of life – reflecting the predominantly ethical character of contemporary philosophy. Interest in the life of Jesus arose from the sense that he provided a way of life – or indeed a pattern of death – to be followed.

The earliest text we have telling the story of a martyr is *The Martyrdom of Polycarp*.[21] Clearly this was written to show that nearly all the events came to pass in order that the Lord should again provide an example which resembles the Gospel story: Polycarp waits to be betrayed, as the Lord was; predicts the manner of his death; refuses to escape, saying, 'God's will be done', and at his trial at first makes no reply; events are narrated that recall the mocking-scenes in the Gospels; the Proconsul parallels Pilate; the crowds behave like the crowds in the passion story; the language of sacrifice describes Polycarp's burning on the pyre, and there are eucharistic allusions as the flames surround him like bread being baked. Many early Christian texts suggest that martyrdom could be called the 'baptism in blood' and was thought to purify from post-baptismal sin, and indeed, even to expiate the sins of others.[22] So the passion story was exemplary, as the martyrs entered the 'mopping-up operation' against the powers of evil, though the victory was in principle already won by Christ.[23] Origen could speak of the sacrifice of the martyrs as parallel to the sacrifice of Christ, equally predicted in the types and symbols of the Law.[24]

With the conversion of Constantine, martyrdom was replaced by monasticism – here was a similar kind of self-sacrificial struggle against the powers of evil.[25] Christ became the model of chastity, virginity or celibacy. This way of life was already an ideal in the second century – the Apologists drew attention to the sexual abstinence practised by Christians. In the fourth century, as we have explored in an earlier chapter, Christians stepped across the line between the desert and the place of settlement and cultivation, following the Christ who had no home and remained unmarried, and the purity and virginity of his mother was a further endorsement. If the body was a temple of the Holy Spirit, it had to be kept pure and undefiled. The Desert Fathers practised the humble way of Christ, the way of poverty and charity modelled on the Beatitudes.[26]

According to John Chrysostom,[27] the great Golden-mouthed preacher, Christ wished to instruct in all virtue, teaching both by word and by deed, because that is the best method. In words he commands people to be lowly-minded and meek, and then demonstrates this with the washing of the feet. He commands people in words to pray for their enemies and then on the cross says, 'Father, forgive them'. He tells the disciples to take no gold or silver in their purse, training them for poverty by word and by his example: 'Foxes have holes, birds of the air have nests, but the Son of Man has nowhere to lay his head.' In teaching us to pray he includes 'lead us not into temptation', and himself prays, 'Father, if it is possible, let this cup pass away from me' – so showing saints that they should not plunge into dangers. Yet he also says, 'Not as I will, but as Thou wilt', demonstrating acceptance. He prayed as a human being to instruct us and deliver us from pride, to teach self-restraint and submission to God's will. For Chrysostom, Paul's thorn in the flesh had the same function, and time and again in his *Panegyrics on Paul* he recalls Paul's words, 'Be imitators of me, as I am of Christ!'

This ethical ideal was reinforced, of course, by the fact of incarnation. The example of the Christ who humbled himself and, though in the form of God, became incarnate for our sakes, even dying on a cross (in other words, the pattern of Phil. 2), was powerful from early on. *1 Clement* 16 cites Isaiah 53 to show Christ as an example of humble-mindedness to be imitated, along with Psalm 22. But that takes us away from interest in the earthly Jesus as such!

The Fathers show most interest in the earthly life of Jesus when aspects of it became contentious. We have already observed this by giving priority to the anti-docetic motive, one that did not disappear with time. We have just drawn material from a homily of Chrysostom's directed against Marcionites and Manichees, two groups to which docetic ideas were attributed: obviously Christ could only be a moral exemplar if he was truly human and lived a truly human life. It is not surprising that the christological debates of the fourth and fifth centuries focused on particular aspects of the life of Jesus, as they struggled with the Gospel narratives, trying to distinguish what he did as God and what he did as man. Inevitably the problem of the incarnation led to interest in the details of his human existence: eating, sleeping, getting tired, suffering, and so on. The Philippians 2 passage suggested that he took the form of a servant, and this, some insisted, was the way to interpret John 1:14, 'the Word became flesh'; it was inappropriate to attribute change to the divine. Cyril of Alexandria[28] opposed the implied dividing of the Christ into divine and human natures, and as a way of preserving the unity of the Christ, fastened on another aspect of the passage from Philippians 2, the *kenōsis* theme:

> He who is from above, and is by nature the only-begotten Son of God the Father, *emptied himself* and was brought forth from a virginal womb according to the flesh ... You will call his name Emmanuel: that is, you will acknowledge that God has appeared in human form.[29]

Thus he emphasised Christ's voluntary self-emptying for us, insisting that his self-emptying was not sufficient to overwhelm his divinity – indeed, it was self-chosen out of his love for us: he humiliated himself voluntarily. It is only because he humbled himself willingly that we may become 'sons of God' by grace. Cyril suggests that he appears 'to fall short of God's majesty by becoming a fully human being', but he insists that the Godhead is in no way diminished by this chosen path of humiliation. 'He brought himself down to that which he was not for our sake.'[30] 'He made the limitations of humanity his own.'[31] For Cyril, Adam was disobedient and in his pride sought to be like God, which led to the Fall; whereas Christ was obedient, and emptied himself in humility that we might be made divine. The important thing was that this enabled the divine life that was in Christ to be inserted into us, 'mingled with our bodies'.[32] The flesh of the Saviour is life-giving,

> And when we taste of it we have life within ourselves, since we too are united with the flesh of the Saviour in the same way as that flesh is united with the Word that dwells with it.[33]

So the Eucharist 'will certainly transform those who partake of it and endow them with its immortality.' Thus Cyril picks up the idea already expressed by Ignatius in the second century that the Eucharist is the 'medicine of immortality'. Life is hidden away in us like a glowing ember, or some vital nucleus that destroys every trace of corruption in us.[34] The indwelling Spirit is the means whereby Christ accomplished our cleansing and sanctification, endowing us with new life. Now all this depends on the reality of the incarnation: the real flesh of Christ imparted through the real body of Christ in the eucharistic elements.

To sum up then, the human historical Jesus was vital to the Fathers, but they had a very different interest from the modern 'Quest for the Historical Jesus' in the nineteenth and twentieth centuries. Their interest was much more like that of the hymn with which we began, interest in the total over-arching story, which points beyond itself, revealing God's accommodation to the human level for our sake. As we have seen, central to this was Philippians 2:5-11:

> Let the same mind be in you that was in Christ Jesus, who, though he was in the form of God did not regard equality with God as something to be exploited, but emptied himself, taking the form of a slave, being born in human likeness. And being

found in human form, he humbled himself and became obedient to the point of death – even death on a cross . . .

The way of Jesus was the way of *kenōsis*, and the Spirit of Jesus would produce the fruits listed in Galatians 5:22: love, joy, peace, patience, kindness, generosity, faithfulness, gentleness, self- control. These perceptions, I suggest, are very important pointers to where we should look to find signs of God in our world, and are also keys to a biblical spirituality.

2. What can we learn about the Way of Jesus from this exploration of the Fathers?

First of all, reviewing the Fathers' interest in the earthly life of Jesus may put the so-called 'Quest for the Historical Jesus' into perspective. It is not illegitimate – indeed, it may be regarded as the equivalent, for contemporary apologetic, to the Fathers' resistance to docetism. Certainly, the outside world generally assumes that Christians believe in some kind of demigod when they speak of Jesus as God's Son, and among believers the perennial tendency is to make Jesus superhuman.[35] An important corrective is to engage in the process of seeking to discover the Jesus of history under the layers of legend and creed. Furthermore, given that we are ourselves shaped by the mind-set of our own period, we are bound to be intrigued by the question of what is fact and what is fiction,[36] or driven by sheer curiosity about this figure who has had such an influence on history. Modernity has ensured that history matters to us, and in any case, the truth that Jesus lived an earthly life is important to the fundamentals of Christianity. Yet in the end, Christianity stands and falls not on the reconstruction of a detailed account of Jesus' life and teaching, but on the genuine humanness of the life lived, the death died and the 'new creation' effected through the incarnation and resurrection of one affirmed as Son of God. The pattern which was so important to the Fathers is absolutely basic. The way of Jesus reveals a human life of self-emptying, which reflects the divine self-emptying in creation and redemption. The twentieth-century mystic Simone Weil may again help us to grasp this. We noted in the last chapter that she spoke of creation being an act of abandonment – for the infinite God had to withdraw in order to allow something other than the divine self to exist at all. So the *kenōsis* of the incarnation reflects the *kenōsis* of creation, and this divine self-emptying is demonstrated on the cross, in the redemptive 'Godforsakenness' of Jesus Christ.

But there is more we need to learn from the Fathers. We need both to re-engage with the over-arching Christian reading of the Bible, and also to rediscover the way in which our creaturely existence points beyond itself. We will concentrate largely on the latter, since there has been some treatment of the theme of Fall and Redemption in earlier chapters.

Rediscovering how earthly, physical things point beyond themselves

Modernity has had the effect of crippling our attention so that only this world counts. The 'Quest for the Historical Jesus' has focused on precisely what happened during his life as a historical person, and struggles with narratives, such as the transfiguration or the resurrection, which raise questions beyond those historical parameters. In the modern mind-set heaven has been brought to earth. We expect utopia now: if only we can find the right formula, everything can be put to rights – an attitude fed by the real successes of modern medicine. Risk is eliminated by health and safety legislation and people rush to litigation if anything goes wrong. Life has been extended for many of us well beyond the biblical threescore years and ten. Cryogenics offers people the possibility of a return to life if science develops further. The majority even of those who have church funerals have no hope beyond this world. So conditions here are now all important. This deeply affects the churches, which are now afraid of the jibe, 'pie in the sky when you die'. Prayer is focused on what happens in the news media, everyone longs for peace now, and so on . . .

All of this breeds unrealism and anxiety about the human condition.

The Fathers were profoundly aware of our creatureliness, our vulnerability and mortality. Mostly we resist that awareness. Because we have lost touch with the reality of our natural limitations, we cannot discern the paradoxical potential of our ordinary lives to point beyond themselves. I once had an amazing holiday experience, an experience of being human in the natural context of creation, the kind of experience Westerners now rarely have. We were camping and walking in the Okavango Delta. Our guide had an ancient spear and a knife, but for safety we were really dependent upon traditional skills – tracking, observation, caution, keeping the fire alight all night. We didn't see much game, but slid through long, grassy meadows in the punt on a level with frogs and dragonflies, spiders' webs and water-lilies. It was a rich paradise. Yet always the *frisson* of the wild, the edge of insecurity . . . We were little and vulnerable in a stunningly beautiful but potentially threatening world. There was something awesome about just being there. Yet even so, we were cushioned compared with our hunter-gatherer ancestors: we had tinned food and tin-openers, we had insect-repellant and anthisan. We escaped the dreaded malaria and sleeping-sickness, but on our return appreciated the benefit of antibiotics to deal with our tick typhus. And we would escape, flying dramatically over the swamp and seeing the giraffe far below . . . Nevertheless, our experience was a salutary reminder of how artificial our lives have become, and what the human condition really is in the context of creation. In those circumstances you don't question the elephant's right to charge, or the lion's right to pounce; you know you have to let nature be itself and treat it with the appropriate respect, and you also know your own vulnerability. We are limited creatures alongside the rest of creation – indeed, part of the created order. The way of Jesus, in its acceptance of vulnerability and mortality, puts human life into proper perspective, while opening horizons beyond itself.

As already noted, there is a tendency in the modern Quests to try and fit Jesus into categories or types of figure current in the world of his day. In many and complex ways he never quite fits, always bursts the boundaries, whether of prophet, wise man, magician or holy man. The transfiguration and resurrection are essential to the story – explaining away and literalising is not appropriate; for the stories really do flout normal historical categories, and are meant to, without removing, indeed rather enhancing, the significance of this ordinary life, suffering and death – indeed, this apparent defeat which turns out to be victory: for mortality is transformed. We need, surely, to reclaim this dimension fearlessly for biblical spirituality and learn to discern the same 'pointing beyond themselves' in the sacraments – but also in the ordinary everydayness of life. Not for nothing did Jesus eat or go hungry, share in the grief and weeping of his friends as well as their joy. Being in touch with Jesus now means discerning the signs of the life of Jesus in our world.

For me, one of the most important signs is found in the L'Arche communities. The way of Jesus shapes their life. Some 40 or more years ago Jean Vanier invited Raphael and Philippe, men with profound learning disabilities, to leave their institution and live with him. From that tiny beginning, communities have sprung up all over the world where people commit themselves to living in community with some of the most marginalised and damaged people on earth. Over the past 15 years, a group of theologians has met from time to time to reflect on L'Arche and its significance. One fruit of the early meetings was the volume, *Encounter with Mystery – Reflections on L'Arche and Living with Disability*. Since then other papers have been written and circulated around L'Arche Internationale, particularly as they have engaged in reflection on their mission and identity. Let me highlight three aspects of their life which are pointers to the way of Jesus: the sacrament of the bodily and the everyday; the way of *kenōsis*; and the way of trust.

1. First, then, is their sense that physical, everyday reality is a sacrament. Bathing is a particular example: assistants caring for those with the most profound physical and mental disabilities

move from washing an object to discovering a person; they discover the preciousness of the body from recognising that someone's life is in their hands, as touch becomes a sacrament. A few quotations from conversation will illuminate this: 'Through the body we reveal to them that they are precious.' 'Do they discover the love of Jesus through our touch? – Yes, we transmit the presence of Jesus.' Touch becomes a sacrament, as the balance between intimacy and proper respect is reached. It is no wonder that L'Arche has developed foot-washing as a para-liturgy (given that there are difficulties about common participation in the Eucharist since the communities have broken across denominational boundaries); for, just as everyday eating is transfigured in the Eucharist, so the everyday physical reality of human caring is sacramentally taken up into mutual foot-washing.

Latterly I have visited the original L'Arche community in Trosly-Breuil approximately every two years, and have often been welcomed for the Saturday evening meal and prayers at the foyer for those with the most severe disabilities. The first visit in 1993 was deeply transforming. A man with Down's Syndrome sat at my feet, hugged my knees and gazed into my face for hours. His name was Christophe – 'bearer of Christ'. Our mutual contemplation enabled transcendence, and I received from him something that my own profoundly disabled son Arthur had, up to that point, never been able to offer.

Perhaps disillusionment when I next visited that foyer was inevitable. This time it was Edith who had an impact on me. Jean Vanier sometimes quotes Mother Teresa as speaking of the sequence, 'repulsion, compassion, wonderment'. Unfortunately I found myself experiencing Mother Teresa's 'repulsion', as Edith was fed at table, and food and wine ran down her front. Maybe I was meant to realise how some people feel when at table with my son. I was embarrassed and disturbed. But two years later I was back, and finding myself again at the same foyer, I discovered compassion as I held Edith's hands, sitting next to her and endeavouring to ease her self-abuse. Later came the wonderment. Edith had just died. I joined the community 'wake', an evening when people gathered to remember, to tell stories, to testify to Edith's importance to them. Despite the limitations of my French, I found myself in tears. Afterwards I went, with many others who stood and knelt in silence, to see Edith laid out in the chapel at the foyer – the disfigured body, the face at peace, the damaged person at the heart of community – wonderment, transcendence.

Let me share an outline of a biblical reflection developed for L'Arche:

'We have this treasure in earthen vessels' (or clay pots, as modern translations will have it! – 2 Cor. 4:7). Clay pots were used to store all sorts of things in the ancient world – grain, oil, money, even books. Ordinariness was at the heart of the metaphor, with its implied contrast with gold or silver containers. These ordinary pots stand for human bodies, created out of clay, according to Genesis 2, and therefore fragile, vulnerable, potentially broken and not easily put back together. Yet these are the containers of light (think of the pottery lamps used all over the ancient world), and life (God breathed life into the clay figurine that, like a potter, he had moulded), and wisdom (the word for 'treasure' in the Greek Bible almost always refers to wisdom; cf. Col. 2:3 – Christ in whom all the treasures of wisdom and knowledge are hidden).

Our inherent creatureliness is revealed by persons with learning disabilities, whose imperfections challenge a culture obsessed with perfect bodies; witness the cult of sport. L'Arche has discovered beauty in damaged bodies, treasure in vulnerable and fragile persons; this is deeply counter-cultural, but Christ had 'no form nor comeliness' (Isa. 53:2 AV). In the everydayness of attending to bodily functions, feeding and defecating, washing and dressing, the sanctity of bodies is acknowledged, and transformation is found, not in miracles but through recognition of God's love and power in mutual need. In the ordinary, everyday business of living together, the divine image is discerned, secreted in the ordinariness of clay pots that are breakable, but in their brokenness expose the treasure within.

Brokenness and Blessing

L'Arche helps us to see the sacrament of the ordinary and the everyday.

2. The assistants pattern their lives on the self-emptying of Jesus. They give up ambition and the need to chase after success, stooping down to be with the poorest of the poor – like Gandhi cleaning the toilets, engaging with the ordinariness of sweeping floors. This too is deeply counter-cultural. We may be reminded, however, of George Herbert's hymn:

> Who sweeps a room, as for thy laws,
> Makes that and the action fine.
>
> This is the famous stone
> That turneth all to gold;
> For that which God doth touch and own
> Cannot for less be told.

There is here an acceptance of lowliness and fragility, a recognition that Jesus made himself vulnerable and little; and so his followers must learn to live out the Beatitudes, an upside-down world where the poor and the mourners, the meek and the merciful, are blessed.

3. If the assistants reflect the way of Jesus in *kenōsis*, the core members embody the way of trust and simplicity. The first meeting of theologians made a collection of wise sayings at the end of the weekend, and one was, 'They have the capacity to evangelise us.'[37] In our culture, simple trust is not easy and may be seen as sentimental. In fact it is hard won – it contrasts fundamentally with the lack of trust in so many of the institutions of our modern Western society where accountability has become paramount. We sophisticated people can only learn it, and so attain spiritual growth, through receptiveness and mutuality, through the play and laughter which reflects the 'letting go' of anxiety about oneself.

The way of Jesus is the way of trust: 'Consider the lilies of the field and the ravens of the air.' I shall never forget my experience on the Golan Heights. I was with a party visiting an old archaeological site on the flanks of the Heights above the Sea of Galilee. As we left the coach, we were warned to stick to the narrow pathway, as the ground on either side might be mined, and the significance of that was rubbed in at the approach to the site itself, where we passed an old Syrian guard-post. We enjoyed seeing some mosaics from a very early Christian church, and then the party began to move back, but for some reason, I found myself well ahead of the others, traversing that narrow path back on my own.

It was a beautiful afternoon, the sun beginning to drop towards the west over Galilee. The grass was decked with spring flowers – the sheer beauty of nature in the springtime lay around my feet, and I thought of how Jesus, just over the water in Galilee, had also celebrated that beauty: 'Consider the lilies of the field, how they grow; they neither toil nor spin yet Solomon in all his glory was not arrayed like one of these.' The glory of the spring flowers, Jesus suggests, is a reason for absolute trust in the Creator. And how we need that trust – for in that moment on the Golan Heights I remembered also the buried mines beneath the flowers, and the horror of it made me realise, as perhaps never so starkly before, that Jesus came into the same kind of awful world as we live in! The land was occupied by the Romans – the people were oppressed by foreigners or suffering under the rule of client kings. There were quisling officials and terrorists who claimed to be freedom fighters – a generation later the whole thing would explode into uprising and war. Jesus came into a world in turmoil, just like ours. And he got caught up in it – arrested as a challenge to the authorities, the victim of horseplay by the troops guarding him, subjected to summary trials while his associates deserted and denied him, condemned to the Roman punishment of crucifixion. The story is perennial. But he taught us to live with trust. The wilderness way of trust, the way of wrestling Jacob – those patterns we have already explored in the Old Testament – come together as we rediscover how the physical, earthly things of life and the Scriptures point beyond themselves.

Brokenness and Blessing

The Fathers were all too aware of changeability, corruptibility, mortality – all aspects of creatureliness, and they struggled with the notion that God could be involved in all this. Yet they became increasingly realistic about it, indeed increasingly celebrated the reality of the incarnation, the ordinary, everyday life of Jesus, including suffering and death, and began to recognise the positive value of change, for inherent in change is the potential for progress in the moral and spiritual life. The problem with the notion of static perfection is that the only possible change is negative; but Gregory of Nyssa, you may recall from Chapter 1, suggests that life is a kind of mountain climb – there's always more, constant unending progress as we stretch out to what is ahead – *epektasis*. This progress was made possible for us by the genuine human living of one who really was God, transforming our mortality by his life and death.

So L'Arche becomes a sign, allowing us to begin to reclaim the ways in which the life of Jesus points beyond itself.

Re-engaging with the over-arching Christian reading of the Bible

In addition to being limited, we are flawed – we do not live up to our own standards, let alone God's, either as individuals, or as groups, or as the human race as a whole. Modernity has not much liked the doctrine of original sin, which is ironic, given the dreadful events of the twentieth century. A spirituality congenial to our modern or post-modern mind-set, a spirituality focused on self-fulfilment, carries yet more unrealism about the human condition. The approach of the Fathers suggests we need to re-engage with the over-arching Christian reading of the Bible.

In the earliest centuries there was real tension about the Scriptures. Marcion thought the Jewish Scriptures, which we now call the Old Testament, should be rejected; the so-called Gnostics reinterpreted those Scriptures in accordance with their spiritualising doctrines. In the face of this, Irenaeus and others began to affirm lists of books that were read as Scripture in the churches around the world, and to summarise a 'Rule of Faith' which gave the right way to read them. Eventually, out of this process would emerge the creeds. Crucial points were discerned along the way:

- God the Creator and God the Redeemer were not different gods opposed to one another.
- The creation belongs to the one true God and is not the result of a pre-cosmic accident or fall; it was humankind which made wrong choices.
- The story of the Bible is that of the one true God, who created everything and then sought restoration, providentially preparing redemption through the prophets, and in the fullness of time sending the Son of God into the world as a human creature to reverse what had gone wrong.

So Fall and Redemption, a theme we have already explored a bit, became the over-arching story of the Scriptures, read as a unity. The pattern also explained the story of Jesus and the salvation he effected.

Again the theme of *kenōsis* becomes central. For there is a profound contrast between Adam's need to know, his grasping at the tree of knowledge, and the humility of the one who took the opposite route of self-emptying. The theme is symbolised in the Tower of Babel, reversed by Pentecost, and by many other linked narratives across the Scriptures, such as: the Israelites bitten by the snakes of worldly wisdom in the wilderness – hungry, they yearn for the fleshpots of Egypt (Num. 21); yet the bronze serpent signifying divine Wisdom brings healing, and Christ when lifted up on the cross plays the same role (John 3:14); and so the foolishness of God overcomes the wisdom of the world (1 Cor. 1:18ff).

Fall and Redemption are central to the Fathers' reading of the Gospel narrative. For us it is counter-cultural to dwell on human gone-wrongness, and humility is a virtue despised. Yet this gone-wrongness is so evident in the way the world is. Greek tragedy depicted the *hybris* of the hero, that overweening challenge to the gods resulting from heroic success, and resulting in a fall; the Fathers saw that human pride overcome by humility. Maybe we can discern the equivalent when the temptation to control is humbled by learning how to trust, when power gives way to weakness, and those who are successful in worldly terms step down the ladder in imitation of Christ's *kenōsis*.

So to sum up: a biblical spirituality enters into the world of the Psalms, accepting the reality of anguish and anger, wickedness and violence, in oneself and in humanity, yet with the confidence (trust) that God is merciful, and God can transform; for Christ has reversed the disobedience of Adam, and we can have this mind which was in Christ Jesus, namely the mind to live the way of *kenōsis* rather than self-aggrandisement. This involves a radical shift in values. 'Glory' comes not through success – prowess in sport, business, politics or academia – but through humility, through the *kenōsis* of the martyr, the monk, the L'Arche assistant, a *kenōsis* which germinates the fruits of the Spirit. This is possible because God loved us first – that is what our opening hymn celebrates. It is only as we are able to become receptive of God's grace, often mediated through discernment of its presence in others, that we can discover the way of Jesus and the fundamental shape of a biblical spirituality.

Many years ago I had been invited to share with the Othona community for a week.[38] Each morning and evening we gathered for prayers in the oldest place of Christian worship in England still in use, St Peter's on the Wall, at Bradwell in Essex. My disabled son, Arthur, was with me, and so each morning and evening members of the community helped with humping Arthur's wheelchair across the fields. As usual, it was impossible to keep him quiet – he gets especially excited where there is a good echo! But he loves music, and usually listens. One evening the person leading the prayers had planned that we simply sat in silence, but he recognised it was impossible with Arthur present. So he suggested that we create silence by singing Psalms. We sang one of the Othona Psalms after another. We reached one, their version of Psalm 131, that went like this:

I am too little, Lord,
   to look down on others.

I've not chased great affairs
   nor matters beyond me.

I've tamed my wild desires
   and settled my soul.

My soul's a new-fed child
   at rest on the breast.

My brothers seek the Lord,
   both now and for ever.

Suddenly Arthur became the Christ-figure in our midst.

Chapter 4

STRANGERS AND EXILES

Glorious things of thee are spoken,
Zion, city of our God;
He whose word cannot be broken
Formed thee for his own abode.
On the Rock of Ages founded,
What can shake thy sure repose?
With salvation's walls
  surrounded,
Thou mayest smile at all thy foes.

See! The streams of living waters,
Springing from eternal love,
Well supply thy sons and
  daughters,
And all fear of want remove;
Who can faint, while such a river
Ever flows their thirst to assuage –
Grace, which like the Lord, the
  giver,
Never fails from age to age?

Saviour, if of Zion's city
I, through grace, a member am,
Let the world deride or pity,
I will glory in thy name.
Fading is the worldling's pleasure,
All his boasted pomp and show;
Solid joys and lasting treasure
None but Zion's children know.

The hymn owes much to biblical visions, contrasting as it does
the commonwealth of God with the world, an eternal city with
the fading glories pursued on earth, and emphasising citizenship
in heaven through grace. It shares much, apart from its brevity,
with the vast, great work of Augustine, *The City of God*, especially its climactic vision of resurrected life in the new Jerusalem,
where God will be all in all – the source of all satisfaction, life,
health, food, wealth, glory, honour, peace and every blessing.
Both derive material from the Bible – the prophecies of Isaiah
and the visions of the book of Revelation particularly, set in an

overall sense of what the Bible is about. This creates a picture of the Christian having citizenship in the heavenly country, not on earth, in the City of God, not Rome – in other words, being an exile or 'resident alien' in the kingdoms of the world.

To reclaim this biblical theme in an age when religion in many parts of the world is too closely associated with ethnic identity or nationalism, too easily corrupted into a cause of violence and atrocity, would seem to be profoundly important. I think of the general resurgence of religion in Eastern Europe, especially Serbia and Russia, where I have seen the extraordinary rebuilding of vast cathedrals as Orthodoxy is re-embraced as a nationalist heritage. I hardly need mention the Middle East, or the dangerous confrontation between a fundamentalist Christian West and militant Islam. But it also impinges on attitudes nearer home, to the problems of welcoming people who are different to live next door, and to the recurrent resistance to asylum-seekers. I say 'recurrent' because it was happening in Britain 100 years ago, just the same: on 10 May 2004, around the time when these lectures were delivered, the *Guardian* published an article with the headline, '150,000 desperate foreigners risk everything to come to Britain. Newspapers call them a menace. Doomsayers warn millions more will flood in. And it all happened 100 years ago.' A truly biblical spirituality will be shaped by perspectives that challenge current attitudes and behaviours, without being a reversion to otherworldliness or sectarianism. Citizenship of heaven has profoundly earthly implications.

To explore these ideas, we will first engage with Augustine's *The City of God*, and then suggest particular ways in which the biblical theme of the exile or outsider might be embraced positively in our contemporary world.

1. Augustine's City of God

Augustine's study of the City of God amounts to 22 books – in the Pelican English translation it comes to 1090 pages; in other words, it is massive. The key to this enormous work is not fully set out until the end of Book XIV:

> We see then that the two cities were created by two kinds of love: the earthly city was created by self-love reaching the point of contempt for God, the heavenly city by the love of God carried as far as contempt of self. In fact, the earthly city glories in itself, the heavenly city glories in the Lord ... In the former the lust for domination lords it over its princes as over the nations it subjugates; in the other both those put in authority and those subject to them serve one another in love ... The one city loves its own strength shown in its powerful leaders; the other says to its God, 'I will love you, my Lord, my strength'.[1]

Augustine is fond of these rhetorical contrasts, which suggest a dualism. Also, like most political philosophers of antiquity, he easily moves from the individual to society, from the family to the body politic. So earlier (IV.3) he had spoken of the grandeur of the Roman Empire by contrast with the City of God: he likened it to a rich man, tortured by fears, burnt up with ambition, always struggling with opponents, piling up more and more resources, and set it over against someone of only moderate means, content with limited resources, loved by family and friends as well as neighbours, loyal, compassionate and kind. This individual characterisation he projects onto the stage of history, empires and cities, contrasting the drive in this world for victory, high rank, life and peace (which he acknowledges as always the object of war, XIX.12), whereas the aims of the heavenly city are truth, holiness, happiness and eternity. It looks like a sharp dualistic contrast.

But Augustine was well aware that things are more complex than that. He will eventually admit that you cannot simply identify the City of God with the Church, which is a mixed body (XVIII.49); and the Roman Empire is not entirely bad (V.16, 18, 21). It is this realism that makes this enormous work so fascinating. From Book XI onwards he will trace the history of the City of God, which has been on pilgrimage on this earth from the very beginning, but his prime purpose at the start of the work is a response to a huge crisis – the sack of Rome by Attila the Hun in 410 CE, and the consequent accusation that Christianity, by causing the neglect of the gods that made Rome great, was responsible for this disaster. So the first five books are a deconstruction of Roman history, making the following points:

- There were plenty of disasters before the Christianising of the Empire. People always think the disasters of their own time are exceptional and never happened before (IV.1). We might take note of this ourselves: true, the sack of Rome marked the end of an era that had lasted 500 years or more, and true, industrial genocide like the Holocaust never quite happened before; but genocide is not unique, and one needs a longer historical perspective, as Augustine insists.
- It is not so simple as all that, he suggests, to attribute the earlier success of Rome to the Roman gods. Before jumping to that conclusion one has to recognise that disasters happened before the arrival of Christianity, and engage in discussion of further questions: firstly, why the one true God assisted Rome to get an Empire; secondly, what difference the Christian emperors made.
- His answer to the first of those questions is that it is better for a good regime to extend its dominion for the benefit of all, and God recognised some of the virtues of the Romans. To some extent the drive for glory and honour checks the worst excesses of wickedness (V.13), and the Romans provide examples of heroic self-sacrifice for the sake of the state. According to the standards of the earthly city, the Romans have been good – indeed, they may provide an example for Christians to emulate, for how much more should they be prepared to make self-sacrifices for the sake of the City of God (V.18)! So Providence assisted the Romans to attain the glory of so great an Empire, even though it was not based on

the values of the City of God, but rather on greed for glory, and did not even acknowledge the one true God.

- His answer to the second question runs like this: God wanted to show that you did not have to worship false gods to attain the highest office, and so he favoured the first Christian Emperor, Constantine, who was even more successful than the pagan emperors (V.25). But God also needed to ensure that no one was a Christian just for the sake of earthly success; so there were subsequent political problems. In the current Emperor Theodosius, however, a new kind of attitude can be detected – he loved his rivals and enemies with Christian charity, and though the greatest power on earth, he displayed religious humility and did penance for an act of vengeance against the people of Thessalonica (V.26).

In these ways, then, Augustine struggled with the complexities of power and the intermingling of good and bad in history. Rome is not simply treated negatively. God's providence is over good and bad alike. Yet at the core of worldly pomp and glory is something deeply at odds with the values of God's commonwealth.

As indicated, from Book XI onwards the earthly history of the City of God is traced, and for much of the time Augustine finds it easy to track its citizens within the story of the Bible. It is from Scripture we learn that there is a City of God, he says, and how the two cities, earthly and heavenly, are intertwined. Time and again he brings out the contrasts: humanity is social by nature, but quarrelsome by perversion (XII.28), so the earthly city is characterised by jealousy and quarrelling, while the City of God is founded on love of God and neighbour (XIV.4). Cain and Abel embody this contrast (XV.1), and this highlights an important point for our theme: Abel is a pilgrim, while Cain settled down and founded a city (XV.1). Time and again the City of God, as traced by Augustine, is said to be on an earthly pilgrimage. The citizens of the City of God are restored to health, while on pilgrimage on this earth, by keeping Gospel precepts about mutual forgiveness (XIV.9); but all the time they sigh for their heavenly country (XV.6). The Church proceeds on its pilgrim way in these evil days, says Augustine, but its troubled course did not just begin with the bodily presence of Christ and in the time of the apostles – it started with Abel, the first righteous man slain by an ungodly brother, and pilgrimage goes on from that time right up to the end of history, with the persecutions of the world on one side, and on the other, the consolations of God (XVIII.51).

Introducing his theme right at the start (I.Preface), Augustine had spoken of the City of God in two aspects, 'as it exists in this world of time, a stranger among the ungodly, living by faith' and 'as it stands in the security of its everlasting seat' (I.9). Christians are those who are 'strangers in this world and fix their hope on a heavenly country'. As early as Book I he calls it 'the pilgrim city of Christ the King' and spells out the ambiguities:

> She [the pilgrim City] must bear in mind that among [her] enemies are hidden her future citizens; and when confronted with them she must not think it a fruitless task to bear with their hostility until she finds them confessing the faith. In the same way, while the City of God is on pilgrimage in this world, she has in her midst some who are united with her in participation in the sacraments, but who will not join with her in the eternal destiny of the saints. Some of these are hidden; some are well-known ... In truth, those two cities are interwoven and intermixed in this era, and await separation at the last judgement. (I.35)

From the beginning, then, Augustine has admitted that the Church is a mixed body, suggesting (XVIII.49) that heresy, like persecution, trains the Church to obey the Gospel precepts, especially those about loving enemies. Interestingly, he also shows some openness to the possibility that there were citizens of the heavenly city outside the race of Israel prior to Christ (XVIII.47), acknowledging the possibility of prophets who do not appear in the scriptural canon, and pointing to Job, 'that holy and amazing man', who was not a native of Israel but an

Brokenness and Blessing

Edomite. So the two cities are mingled together from the beginning to the end of history. Both enjoy the good things and suffer the bad things of this temporal state, but with a different love and a different expectation. They will be separated at the Final Judgement (XVIII.54). The earthly city aims at earthly peace, whereas that part of the heavenly city on pilgrimage in this condition of mortality looks for this kind of peace to pass away. It 'leads what we may call a life of captivity in this earthly city, as in a foreign land' and 'calls out citizens from all nations', collecting 'a society of aliens, speaking all languages' (XIX.17, 27). It is focused on love of God and love of neighbour, and struggles during its pilgrimage to love even its enemies, as commanded by Christ. Augustine's own pretty intolerant life shows how he himself betrayed this vision: he called in state power to deal with the Donatist schismatics, appealing to the text of one of the Gospel parables, 'Compel them to come in'. Yet, as we have seen, he displays considerable sensitivity to the complexities of power and the ambiguities of history.

So perhaps we can learn something from the vision of history he has developed. It was, of course, rooted in his own time; there are pages and pages about pagan religion and philosophy, which we will hardly find relevant. Nevertheless, this work may yet distil a vision, which he has developed from the visions of Scripture, which could be significant for us in a profoundly different situation. Although the translation quoted has not used the word 'exiles', it is this that sums up Augustine's sense of the life of Christians on earth: their citizenship belongs elsewhere, and like the Jews of the Diaspora, they look to another country as their home.

So who are the exiles in our time? For liberation theology they are the poor:

> The breakthrough of the poor into Latin American history and the Latin American Church is based on a new and profound grasp of the experience of estrangement. The exploited and marginalized are today becoming increasingly conscious of

living in a foreign land that is hostile to them, a land of death, a land that has no concern for their most legitimate interests and serves only as a tool for their oppressors, a land that is alien to their hopes and is owned by those who seek to terrorize them ... Exiled, therefore, by unjust social structures ... but aware now they've been despoiled of it, the poor are actively entering into Latin American history and taking part in an exodus that will restore to them what is rightfully their own.[2]

But others who have recently explored the question challenge us to reclaim for ourselves the sense of being alien, of being on pilgrimage or living as 'resident aliens' in a strange land, like the citizens of Augustine's City of God. I quote:

'Christianity is an invitation to be part of an alien people.'

'The Church exists today as resident aliens, an adventurous colony in a society of unbelief.'

'Life in the colony is not a settled affair ... The colony is a people on the move ...'

'We serve the world by showing it something that it is not, namely a place where God is forming a family out of strangers.'[3]

These suggestions may in the end have deep connections, but placed starkly side by side, they appear alternatives, and, I would suggest, they do not sufficiently attend to the complexities which Augustine explored. The two cities are intertwined. So who might we identify as 'resident aliens' in our world? How are we to embrace this biblical model in our spirituality?

2. Embracing a biblical theme

At this point allow me to take an autobiographical turn and divulge how I got fascinated by the biblical theme of the resident alien. Every year the Diploma in Pastoral Studies at the University of Birmingham used to hold a conference, and in 1986 it focused on persons with learning disabilities, their needs and the theological issues surrounding their lives. An Anglican priest, Revd Ian Cohen, presented a paper entitled 'They ... endure all disabilities as aliens'.[4] His paper will take us deeper into the biblical development of this theme.

Cohen confessed himself the father of a son with severe epilepsy, who as a result of his constant fits was gradually losing brain function and abilities as he grew up. Cohen observed that, like liberation theology, biblical studies concerned with a theology of disability tended to focus on the 'marginalised', 'the poor' or 'disadvantaged'. But these images are of people who can be integrated if circumstances are changed; with the right kind of social organisation the economically poor need not be so. Cohen proposed the biblical *gēr* or 'resident alien' as a more appropriate term for consideration when looking for a biblical model for those whose condition cannot be changed – that is, the 'sojourner', a 'protected or dependent foreigner', a 'protected stranger ... of another tribe or district, coming to sojourn in a place where he was not strengthened by the presence of his own kin, who put himself under the protection of a clan or a powerful chief'.

Cohen proceeded to give an account of the status of such a sojourner in early Israelite law: neither an Israelite nor a slave, he was bound to respect the Sabbath, this being a privilege, to gain rest and refreshment. The *gēr* was to be treated fairly and protected against injustice and violence. And the reason for this was that the *gēr* reflected the true soul of the Israelite, and enabled the Israelite to recollect the feelings of the *gēr*:

> You shall not wrong a *gēr* or be hard on him; you were *gērim* yourselves in Egypt ... You shall not oppress the *gēr* for you know how it feels to be a *gēr*; you were *gērim* yourselves in Egypt. (Exod. 22:21; 23:9)

Deuteronomy 27:19 puts the *gēr* alongside the orphan and widow as the kind of person for whom Israel was responsible:

A curse on anyone who withholds justice from the *gēr*, the orphan and the widow!

The *gērim* are to receive gleanings, like the widows and orphans.

Cohen went on to show how Abraham is depicted as a *gēr* and how, as the father of the nation, he is a 'type' of what Israel sees to be its own nature. Joseph and his brothers are *gērim* in Egypt and seek Pharaoh's protection. Moses lived as a *gēr* in Midianite territory. Elijah experienced the lot of a *gēr*. In Egypt and the Exodus they had a communal experience of having nowhere to call their own, and in the Promised Land they recited, 'My father was a homeless Aramaean who went down to Egypt . . .', as they gave thanks for the first-fruits. So being a *gēr* was deep in the Israelite identity, and one of the first commandments in Deuteronomy is to love the *gēr* because God is no respecter of persons and loves the alien who lives among you. The prophets pick up the theme, especially Jeremiah, who does not suggest a physical return to Egypt, but does point to rediscovery of the soul of the *gēr* as important. He experiences being an 'outsider' himself because of his terrible message, and even hints that God would be 'as a *gēr*' (14:8). The person who is different, the literal stranger, the 'other', is thus a sign of what Israel truly is, and as the prophet steps into that place, he is also a sign of God's otherness, God's strangeness. There is a belonging which is also not a belonging.

For Ian Cohen this illuminated the strange belonging yet not belonging of the 'alien' child in the family, the strange child who is different, though 'bone of my bone and flesh of my flesh'. But it also points to the connection between the two interpretations briefly outlined earlier: the poor and marginalised may justifiably identify with Israel as *gēr* in Egypt and hope for their Exodus, but we, as affluent, settled Israelites, also need to remember that that is our soul, and that this has consequences for our way of being in society. Conversely, Jeremiah told the exiles to build houses and dig gardens in a foreign land. Even if the Church seems to be in exile in a post-Christian society, life goes on, and withdrawal into a ghetto mentality is not the biblical way. Being 'in the world' but not 'of the world' is a complex matter, as Augustine had already found in his own explorations of the same sort of biblical material.

But to return to Cohen's paper – he then embarks on a study of the New Testament, especially 1 Peter. The author implies that the Church is a new Israel, a nation of sojourners: 'Beloved, I urge you as aliens and exiles to abstain from the desires of the flesh ... Conduct yourselves honourably among the Gentiles, so that, though they malign you as evil-doers, they may see your honourable deeds and glorify God' (2:11–12). Christians may be ethnically related to their pagan neighbours, but they have become different – aliens and exiles, sojourners, resident aliens, *paroikoi* (to use the Greek term). 'Live in reverent fear during the time of your exile' (1:17), as you invoke the Father who judges all impartially. Cohen shows how this was expanded in some of the earliest Christian writings outside the New Testament, especially the *Epistle to Diognetus*, from which he took the title of his paper. It is worth exploring this epistle a bit further, especially to observe the extent to which it is a precedent for Augustine's outlook.

The author insists that Christians are not distinguished from the rest of humankind by country, speech or customs, yet, while conforming to everyone else in dress, food, mode of life, and so on, they live as aliens, sharing in everything as citizens, and enduring everything as foreigners. The author loves the rhetoric that sharpens up this point: 'Every foreign land is their fatherland, yet for them every fatherland is a foreign land.' They busy themselves on earth, but their citizenship is in heaven. They obey the established laws, but go far beyond them in their own lives; they love all but by all are persecuted; they are dishonoured but glorified in their dishonour; they are reviled, yet they bless – the rhetoric of contrast is developed at length.

But the point for Cohen is the continuation of biblical ideas in early Christianity – and we have seen it even later and more developed in Augustine. Christians live as strangers and exiles on earth. Cohen notes that the Risen Christ is accused of being a *paroikos* in the story of the walk to Emmaus; and the Psalms which speak of being a *gēr* (e.g. Ps. 39) have their parallels in the passion-narratives. His deduction is that we should not care for those with disabilities because that does us good – that would be patronising charity. Rather, we care for them because they reveal to us who we really are – that is how 'the Other' matters. As *gērim* they show us that we too have the soul of the *gēr*.

3. Welcoming difference

I said this was an autobiographical turn. It was so because Ian Cohen's paper was profoundly important to me in my pilgrimage with my son Arthur. Years later I would write a paper for L'Arche on 'Welcoming Difference'. Slightly adapted, this I now share. I had been asked to speak personally, and in the context of L'Arche that meant as the parent of an adult son who requires total care – who has no self-help skills, no independent mobility, no language. For me it also meant speaking as a theologian and biblical scholar: for, as I explained, my whole being is shaped by theological searching, by seeking to respond to God – a God who is 'the Other', utterly different, yet revealed as one with us in Jesus Christ. The previous chapters thus provide the theological context for the following exploration.

I shared three related reflections on welcoming difference: the last offered some personal testimony, the second was a Bible study, the first attempted some honest appraisal of our human condition. The burden of what I had to say is that we should never imagine that it is easy to welcome difference; yet it is wonderfully enriching, lies at the heart of the Gospel and deepens worship and spirituality.

Welcoming difference: the challenge and the prize

Human creatures are not naturally inclined to welcome difference. Once I was driving Arthur through some lanes just outside our home city of Birmingham. At one point we came round a corner to see a horse straining at the reins as the dismounted rider tried to steer it reluctantly along the road. I stopped the car and we waited. As they went past, the girl said, 'She can't stand the Shetlands.' It took me a moment to realise what she meant. Over the hedge in the field were several tiny little shaggy Shetland ponies. It seemed the horse recognised that they were the same but different, and so found them scary and threatening.

That seemed to me a parable of how human beings actually react to one another. Throughout history, race, ethnicity and other differences have generated reaction against people seen as alien, strange, threateningly different – yet the same. The period of the slave trade, I discover, generated a sense of the European having a dark twin, the African, and needing to subjugate, even kill this challenging double.

Religious differences have compounded reaction against 'the other', and paradoxically the bitterest conflicts are often between those who are most alike: Eastern Orthodox Christians parted company with Western Catholics in the Middle Ages; Catholics rejected the prophetic voice of Protestants at the Reformation; Anglicans found John Wesley far too hot to handle; and so ecumenism struggles across the divides between people all of whom claim to be Christian. Jews, Christians and Muslims share a common history and heritage, but Christians are blamed by Jews for the Holocaust and by Muslims for the Crusades. So we find ourselves uncomfortable, defensive, threatened by centuries of failure to welcome difference. Indeed, not only is Europe's history marred by religious wars, but the major conflicts we now see on our television screens have religious dimensions: the Middle East, India and Pakistan, the former Yugoslavia, Northern Ireland – we could go on. It seems as if the more alike we are, the less able we are to welcome difference.

But the difference in question, in the context of L'Arche and my personal experience, is one hard to name and hard to be honest about. In England the term 'mentally handicapped' is no longer acceptable. There is resistance to naming the difference; for political correctness fosters the worthy aim of avoiding labels and stereotyping. Yet many people cannot help reacting to difference like the horse to the Shetland ponies – so whatever term is used is eventually misused. Once 'retarded' simply described the condition – these people were indeed late developers; but soon the word turned into a term of abuse. This is our dilemma. On the one hand, it is now correct to talk of 'people with learning difficulties', to reduce the difference, to try and avoid a 'them and us' mentality – for we all have learning difficulties, even though we may be professors at university! On the other hand, the kind of support and affirmation that people like my son need requires a naming of difference, and it is impossible to deal with the realities by taking what, in the context of racial discrimination, would be called the 'colour-blind' approach.

Besides, it is not just a matter of sanitising the language. I have heard parents confess to never taking a holiday because they could not face the embarrassment of people's stares when they go to the beach. People in society react with varying degrees of shock, rejection or patronising compassion to people who are different in this way. If I am honest as a parent myself, I have to acknowledge having had powerful conflicting emotions about my son, who is flesh of my flesh but not like me, not at all like his adult younger brothers who are both now fathers – Arthur has long since been overtaken by his own niece and nephews in language and understanding, skills and capabilities. It is no good pretending there is no difference. If we are to welcome difference, to affirm the 'other' and embrace the stranger, we have to acknowledge first that there *is* a difference.

Some years ago I found the work of the anthropologist Mary Douglas helpful for analysing the issues raised by difference. In her book *Purity and Danger*, the starting-point is the observation that every society has 'purity' regulations – every human culture distinguishes between what is clean and what is not. Dirt, she says, implies a 'set of ordered relations and contravention of that order'. 'Dirt is the by-product of a systematic ordering and classification of matter.'[5] Individuals, as they grow up, are encultured into this ordered view of the world: my mother told me my first words were 'pretty' and 'dirty'.

The ordered system whereby the world is classified, known and understood, however, is inevitably challenged by what Douglas calls 'anomalies' and 'ambiguities' – things that do not fit predetermined categories. Her argument is that the desire for purity proves to be 'hard and dead', that 'purity is the enemy of change'.[6] The crucial thing is how a society copes with anomalies. It may exclude them, or seek to interpret them within the system. Or it may respond so as to generate something creative. The things that do not fit, the marginal or liminal, may produce revulsion, shock or laughter, but may also provoke novelty. Religious ritual, she suggests, is a way of dealing with taboo and terrible things so as to produce cleansing and new life.[7] She suggests a parable (mentioned before in Chapter 1): the gardener tidies, orders, or, we might say, 'purifies' the garden by taking out the weeds. If the weeds are burned or thrown away, that is that. But if the weeds are turned into compost, then the 'anomalies' become life-giving. So animal sacrifice turned the taboo substance, blood, into a life-giving and atoning reality.

So to the point: human societies do not naturally welcome difference. Our hunter-gatherer ancestors could not afford to support anyone infirm or incapable, whether through age, injury or disability. They had to find ways of reinterpreting the birth of an 'anomaly', to deal with the challenge and shock. Mary Douglas gives an example from the Nuer tribe:

> when a monstrous birth occurs, the defining lines between humans and animals may be threatened. If a monstrous birth can be labelled an event of a peculiar kind the categories can be restored. So the Nuer treat monstrous births as baby hippopotamuses, accidentally born to humans, and with this labelling, the appropriate action is clear. They gently lay them in the river where they belong . . .

Societies in the grip of high modernity did something somewhat similar when they employed the medical model as a way of justifying the exclusion of people with disabilities into hospitals. The early twentieth-century fascination with genetic purity reinforced that and led to the Nazi policy of 'cleansing' society of people with defects, as well as those with the 'wrong' ethnicity, like Jews and Gypsies.

But Mary Douglas suggests that such attempts to achieve purity prevent the creative from happening, and that through welcoming difference, profound breakthroughs can occur. It is because we can transcend our natural reactions that we are more than naked apes. It is not natural to choose to live with people who are different, and there are profound challenges involved in doing so. Yet ' "they" have the power to evangelise "us" ' – in other words, the people who are disadvantaged, disabled, poverty-stricken in more ways than one, have the capacity to 'convert' those of us who appear to have capabilities they lack.[8] Welcoming difference enables a transforming mutual relationship.

L'Arche is an important outworking of this, a prophetic beacon for the world, if only the world were capable of discerning it. It substantiates Ian Cohen's insights – you can never remove the difference between 'us' and our strange offspring. Welcoming difference is never easy, but it is wonderfully enriching. It is also Gospel: so to the Bible study.

Welcoming difference: from embarrassment to communion – the Bible study

The story of Mephibosheth may not be familiar, but the passionate relationship between David and Jonathan is well known. Mephibosheth was Jonathan's son. Jonathan was the son of King Saul, but David was anointed to be the next king. Saul's jealousy of David set him on the run. One of the most moving passages in Scripture is David's lament over the deaths of Saul and Jonathan in battle, even though it meant his own accession to the throne (2 Sam. 1). Yet David's advance was bound to be terrifying for the royal house. Jonathan's five-year-old son was picked up by his nurse as she fled. She dropped the child, who was crippled as a result (2 Sam. 4:4). This is a biblical story about someone with disabilities.

Having established his position, David enquired whether there were any of Saul's descendants left – he wanted to show kindness for Jonathan's sake (2 Sam. 9). He was told about Mephibosheth. To him David restored Saul's lands, and made arrangements for Saul's servant, Ziba, to farm them. Then David said to Mephibosheth, 'You will eat at my table.' The sequel reveals that his motives were mixed. He wanted to show kindness, yet he needed to keep an eye on a potential rival, and having him eat at the king's table was a good way of doing it. The evidence lies in the fact that during Absalom's revolt David's suspicions were aroused by Mephibosheth's failure to retreat from Jerusalem with him. In fact, Ziba played on David's fears, suggesting that Mephibosheth hoped to receive the kingdom as a result of the revolt (2 Sam. 16:1–4). Mephibosheth was dispossessed and Ziba got the land.

The revolt was eventually crushed, and Mephibosheth came with many others to pay homage to David (2 Sam. 19:24ff). He was dishevelled and unwashed, explaining that he had tried to follow David. He had called for his donkey to be saddled, but Ziba had betrayed him, depriving a cripple of his wheelchair-equivalent! David's reaction was ambiguous – he did not know who to trust. Yet when a hostile neighbouring tribe demanded the death of all Saul's descendants, David 'spared Mephibosheth, the son of Saul's son Jonathan, because of the oath of the Lord that was between David and Jonathan, son of Saul' (2 Sam. 21:7). So was it after all his love of Jonathan that had motivated his support for Mephibosheth?

Taken as a whole, this story provides powerful insight into a confusion of good and bad motives, fraught relationships, the interplay between power and powerlessness on both sides. Mephibosheth was marginalised by the political situation, but also by his disability. He became a recipient of patronage and charity, sitting on the fringes, lacking position and dignity. But David meant to be kind because of his love for Jonathan. So

Mephibosheth was marginalised by David's mixed feelings – sentiment for Jonathan coupled with suspicion because of Saul. But David was wrong-footed because his own position was vulnerable. Strange that a quirk of history means that Mephibosheth's name includes the word for 'shame'.[9]

Now to make an unexpected correlation! Eating at the king's table might be a way of describing the Eucharist, and if there was less than perfect communion between David and Mephibosheth as they ate together, the same was true of the church in Corinth. They were finding it very hard to welcome difference: there were splits, suspicions, denigrations, marginalisations damaging the community. Were the divisive issues doctrinal or economic or social? We simply do not know. Nor does it matter for the link between the old story about David and Paul's pleas with his congregation. In 1 Corinthians 11 he rehearses the story of the Last Supper in order to challenge the way the Corinthian church was behaving when they met and ate together.

In the following chapter we find Paul's famous description of the body of Christ. Here we discover that 'shame' is another link: the head cannot say to the feet, 'I don't need you!'

> On the contrary, those parts of the body that seem to be weaker are indispensable, and the parts that we think are less honourable we treat with special honour. And the parts that are unpresentable are treated with special modesty … (1 Cor. 12:21b–23a)

The word translated 'unpresentable' means any of the following: deformed, ugly, unseemly or shameful. In other words, as Paul unfolds his metaphor, he refers to the ugly bits we want to hide, the private parts we usually cover up in public – the body-bits that people in most societies throughout history have been ashamed of or embarrassed about. Paul is demanding that our shame be given dignity – that we do not use fig-leaves any more, so reversing Adam's fall. But of course, he is not really talking about the body literally: he is talking about the community of the body of Christ.

Brokenness and Blessing

Dare we give greater honour to those who cause us shame or embarrassment? People with learning disabilities are the ones whom many societies have wanted to conceal – the difference is too challenging to cope with. In these days of community care, no one wants such people to live in their nice residential neighbourhood, because they'll bring down the property values. In Britain a disturbing number of them are in prison or homeless, begging on the streets. Some are people whose inability to communicate or whose slobbering over their food makes so-called 'decent' people feel uncomfortable, especially at table. And Christians are not immune from challenge: many are embarrassed because they cannot turn them into miracle-fodder – for their disabilities are never healed.

These are the Mephibosheths of modern societies – for people are not really hard-hearted. Indeed, they have a kind of sympathy for them, and are horrified about conditions in Romania's orphanages, while not being prepared to pay taxes to support their own grown-ups with similar impairments. People have powerful mixed emotions. People are like David. They do not know how to react . . .

Well, maybe Paul did not have this particular issue in mind! But the general point about finding it hard to welcome those who are different, especially when it makes us feel shame, remains. So back to 1 Corinthians: in chapter 11, Paul is bothered because he has heard that when they come together as a church there are differences. The rich go ahead and eat without waiting for the poor. Reminding them of what happened at the Last Supper, he warns that whoever eats the bread and drinks the cup without discerning the Lord's body, eats and drinks judgement on themselves. The story of David and Mephibosheth exposed the fact that we can sit at the same table without being in communion. Here such exposure is a kind of judgement. It is to share Adam's shame and mortality. We need the person at the margins – to help us confront our failure.

But Paul sees the death of Christ as potentially transforming relationships at table. Christ, the new Adam, can take away the fig-leaves so that we are not ashamed any more, but capable of welcoming those we feel confused about and eating with them. That is the Gospel that emerges when we put these two passages together.

Ecumenically, we are still wearing fig-leaves. As members of a society divided by privilege and by race, we are still wearing fig-leaves. These are the obvious challenges that Paul presents. But what about people born with learning disabilities? Can the Church rejoice in their fellowship? Or do people feel they should be fed separately? Let me affirm the many open congregations which have welcomed my son Arthur over the years. But the welcome is sometimes patronising, and I know of nice, well-meaning people who are offended by his presence at table and others who are disturbed by his inarticulate shouting in church. Acute embarrassment has been the lot even of those who have loved him, like my own father, sometimes even myself.

For me, one of the signs of the kingdom is to be found in the L'Arche communities. Here we find people who have perceived that welcoming difference lies at the heart of the Gospel, and that it's played out in the ordinariness of eating together.

Welcoming difference – responding to God's Otherness

The journey of my life, with Arthur and in spite of Arthur, has been akin to the Israelites' 40 years in the wilderness – I refer you back to the first chapter. I would once have spoken of a kind of arrival, a return to faith, a sense of salvation and healing, as if the journey was a linear process with a goal attained: faith rebuilt after years of doubt. My book, *Face to Face*, had that kind of perspective. But now I know that the important thing is the journeying, not the arriving. And now I know also that the wilderness motif is far from negative. In the Bible it is the place both of temptation and of meeting with God. It is a place to return to, not simply escape from. New life is found in daring to move on, to tackle a new stage, not in returning to past high moments or seeking the relief of home-coming. It is being open to meeting the strangeness – welcoming the difference – of others, which allows us glimpses of God's Otherness. Ian Cohen has alerted us not only to the way Israel is told to honour the *gēr*, the resident alien, but also to two further biblical motifs: (1) the way Israel is called to share the soul of the *gēr*, to live as a stranger on earth, to wander in the wilderness; and (2) the way God adopts the character of the *gēr*, the outsider, the one despised and rejected, the one different from our expectations.

Welcoming God's difference deepens spirituality. Welcoming the difference of others deepens the experience of worship. I have already spoken of the moment when I was confronted by God's 'Otherness'. Another significant moment came one Easter-time, in Birmingham's inner city, during my first exposure to pastoral ministry as I prepared for ordination. I had begun to get to know the people who made up the congregation – and I had discovered a community which bridged so many of the differences in our society: black and white, young and old, reasonably affluent and quite poor, wide differences in levels of education, physically robust working people and frail elderly folk and people with various disabilities. For the first time I found myself placing the communion bread in outstretched hands which displayed all those differences. Unexpectedly I had had to take Arthur along. No one had met him before but someone took the initiative and pushed his wheelchair up to the front as people came forward to receive communion. So he was part of it, able to receive a blessing. During that Easter celebration, what I recall vividly is mentally seeing the Lord high and lifted up in the temple. No, I am not really a visionary – it was more Isaiah 6 filling my mind than anything else. But there was a stunning sense of exaltation and of the presence of God where the body of Christ welcomed differences.

I might speak of the shock and wonderment of the ecumenical journeys I have been privileged to make over the years: the pain of being an ordained woman unable to relate to Orthodox priests and theologians, and occasionally the joy of acceptance; and the breaking down of inner and outer barriers on the Faith and Light pilgrimage to Lourdes in 1991. Like everyone else, I am always wanting to domesticate, tame, explain, accommodate, avoid conflict, resist the shock of the unfamiliar, be comfortable and at peace, have things make sense. But I have learned that the spiritual growth points are when all that is broken apart, and I become vulnerable, challenged by difference, ready to respect the other.

That is the kind of brokenness Jean Vanier so often speaks about.[10] Recently I became fascinated by the fraction – the snapping – of the communion wafer. Perhaps the breaking of the body of Christ is necessary for the Church to be the Church. Only after the fraction can the broken pieces be gathered again into the one loaf. As the Spirit of the living God breaks and moulds each of us, so the Church has to suffer the pain of brokenness so as to be humbled and ready to welcome difference. Maybe it is significant that L'Arche and Faith and Light, places where broken people are welcomed, have become also places where ecumenism has become an imperative. Christ had 'no form nor comeliness' – the broken, crucified body was scarcely a pretty sight, hardly something to be welcomed. Those who are different sometimes enable that shock to be felt.

4. Bringing it all together

We have come a long way from Augustine, but the linking theme is the sense of not belonging, of welcoming the stranger in our society because, deep down, we are strangers ourselves. Albert Camus wrote a novel called *The Outsider* – it is the story of someone who did not behave according to convention, did not play the game, a solitary who tells the truth. The author said about it:

> One wouldn't be far wrong in seeing *The Outsider* as the story of a man who, without any heroic pretensions agrees to die for the truth. I ... once said ... paradoxically, that I tried to make my character represent the only Christ that we deserve ... In

the modern world, a truly Christ-like figure would be rejected and his followers would be aliens – as once they were.[11]

A biblical spirituality requires the discovery of the soul of the *gēr* – the stranger within ourselves.

In the second and third centuries Christians were known as the 'Third Race' – neither Jew nor Greek, and they claimed it with pride, picking up the biblical themes of having their citizenship in heaven. Bishop Polycarp died because he refused to say 'Lord Caesar' rather than 'Lord Christ', proudly affirming his allegiance to Christ for 86 years: to that extent Christianity was political, taking over the language of the imperial cult – *euangelion, parousia* and many other terms come directly from that world. The early Church adopted the organisation of the municipality, with its order of clergy and its plebs – the laity or people. In all these ways we can observe it becoming an alternative polity to the Roman Empire, at least until Constantine's conversion. Even then Augustine reclaims this older tradition and refuses the co-inherence of Church and Christian Empire. Yet the Church has never really adopted the soul of the *gēr* to the extent of identifying with those who are 'other' and learning to respect and welcome them, despite the fact that the seeds were there. In addition to the biblical material about the *gēr* which we have been exploring, these seeds may be identified as (1) a recognition of God's single sovereignty over all and divine providence overseeing all; together with (2) the affirmation of Christ as the embodiment of the Logos to be found in the philosophers of the Greeks as well as the prophets of the Jews – so the wisdom of all nations; and also (3) the command to love, loving God embracing the love of brethren, neighbours, and even enemies. We honour and respect the stranger and the exile, because we have the soul of the exile – our citizenship is in heaven, and we know what it means to be away from home.

In *Finding Peace* Jean Vanier, quoting from a letter from Philip Kearney, tells a remarkable story. It is about a group of eight men with severe intellectual and physical disabilities, two being

Palestinian Muslims, three Palestinian Christians, and three Israeli Jews:

> Once a week [writes Philip Kearney] I go for a walk with this strange and wonderful group in the streets and parks ... It's quite an experience. Palestinians who have known them for many years come up and greet them by putting their hands on their heads in a sort of gesture of welcome and blessing. Then a little further on Israelis come up and greet the group, recognizing their own. The joy that these meetings give to those who approach is quite visible. Up until today this is the only group that I have met with representatives of the three great religions of this land not only living together day by day, but also walking hand in hand in the streets of Jerusalem together![12]

Maybe our post-modern, pluralist world is one which requires our reading of Scripture to challenge exclusiveness, to go beyond mere tolerance to respect, to recognise how fundamentally important is the 'Other' for our own identity; and so pick up where Augustine had got to, and then go on to discover that salvation involves breaking us open from security and belonging, in ways he never dreamed of, despite his recognition that the key to the whole Bible was love of God and love of neighbour.[13] A biblical spirituality demands more than self-fulfilment, as one discovers oneself through compassionate and mutual engagement with others, especially those who are different. It is in this way that our citizenship in heaven impinges profoundly on our earthly existence.

Chapter 5

∞∞∞∞∞∞∞∞∞∞∞∞∞∞∞∞∞

DESIRE FRUSTRATED AND FULFILLED

Jesus, lover of my soul,
Let me to thy bosom fly,
While the nearer waters roll,
While the tempest still is high;
Hide me, O my Saviour, hide,
Till the storm of life is past;
Safe into the haven guide,
O receive my soul at last!

Other refuge have I none,
Hangs my helpless soul on thee;
Leave, ah, leave me not alone,
Still support and comfort me.
All my trust on thee is stayed,
All my help from thee I bring;
Cover my defenceless head
With the shadow of thy wing.

Thou, O Christ, art all I want;
More than all in thee I find;
Raise the fallen, cheer the faint,
Heal the sick, and lead the blind.
Just and holy is thy name,
I am all unrighteousness;
False and full of sin I am,
Thou art full of truth and grace.

Plenteous grace with thee is
   found,
Grace to cover all my sin;
Let the healing streams abound,
Make and keep me pure within.
Thou of life the fountain art,
Freely let me take of thee;
Spring thou up within my heart,
Rise to all eternity.

Charles Wesley's hymn draws on a range of biblical imagery, but the overarching feel seems to be captured in the opening lines – the soul rests in Christ as a bride lies in the arms of her bridegroom. This picks up a long-standing theme in Christian devotion. It doubtless came to Charles Wesley from the Puritan tradition. Quoting Richard Sibbes (1577–1635), Gordon Wakefield wrote:

> the Bride is the Church, though since 'all Christian favours belong to all Christians alike ... every Christian soul is the spouse of Christ as well as the whole Church'. The divine

lover's kisses are Christ's presence in the ordinances; the
sacraments are his love tokens.[1]

In the medieval West this theme is best represented by Bernard
of Clairvaux, whose love mysticism found vivid expression in the
visions of medieval women who saw themselves as brides of
Christ and languished in their cots with desire, 'dissolved with
such a particular and marvellous love towards God'.[2] Its long
history has its roots in the period of the Fathers and their exegesis
of the Song of Songs; and they were almost certainly adapting an
already existing Jewish tradition. It is here we will begin our
explorations.

1. Ancient interpretation of the Song of Songs

The Song of Songs and its place in the canon according to Jewish tradition

On the face of it, the Song of Songs is a love poem. Some of it
seems to be a dialogue or drama with different voices speaking. It
would appear to be Solomon's wedding-night, the king and his
bride rejoicing in one another, drawing poetic likenesses, using
metaphors and figures of speech to articulate a sense of beauty
and of joy in each other, the desire to which they are aroused,
their mutual delight. At times the language goes beyond the
merely romantic to the blatantly erotic, but this is obscured by
the majority of published translations. I cite the English translation by Marvin Pope in the Anchor Bible:

> My love thrust his hand into the hole,
> And my inwards seethed for him ...
> I opened to my love ... (5:4, 6)

> Your stature resembles the palm,
> Your breasts the clusters.
> Methinks I'll climb the palm,
> I'll grasp its branches.

Brokenness and Blessing

Let your breasts be like grape clusters,
The scent of your vulva like apples ... (7:8–9)

The language of poetry is always full of metaphor – the literal meaning is never possible, never intended. But modern readings of this text have tended to privilege what might be called the 'obvious' meaning – the surface meaning of the text. So the Song of Songs is taken to be a song of love for Solomon's wedding-night, and the principal problems become (1) who this unknown bride might be, since she is never mentioned elsewhere in Scripture, and (2) how this love-poem ever got into the canon of Scripture. Interestingly, this latter question was clearly raised as early as the first century CE; for Rabbi Aqiba replied:

> No Israelite ever disputed about the Song of Songs ... The whole world is not worth the day on which the Song of Songs was given to Israel, for all the scriptures are holy, but the Song of Songs is the Holy of Holies.[3]

This estimate was based on the assumption that the poem was really about the love affair between God and Israel – an assumption with some justification, given the potential inter-textual links. Hosea made explicit the possibility of speaking about Israel's election in terms of God having chosen a bride from among the nations of the earth. He married a wife and had children; then she was unfaithful and he struggled to win her back – and this became a parable of God's struggles to win back faithless Israel. One kind of covenant was the marriage-bond; so you could tell the story of God's covenant with Israel in terms of a bridegroom with his bride: faithlessness and judgement, love and restoration. This is exactly what we find in the Targum on the Song of Songs.[4]

A Targum is a paraphrastic translation incorporating inter-pretation, and basically what the Targum does is to go through the Song treating it as an oblique account of Israel's history. It is often difficult to see exactly how the Targum relates to the actual Hebrew text of the Song, and at other times the general thrust is almost lost in details intended to reflect the text; but the opening makes clear the intention. Solomon the prophet begins:

> Blessed is the name of the Lord who gave us the Law by the hand of Moses ... and spoke to us face to face as a man kisses his companion, from the abundance of the love with which He loved us, more than the 70 nations ...

(The '70 nations' is the classic expression for the Gentiles.) Then there is traced in the 'under-sense' of the text the story of the Exodus, of the Red Sea crossing, the giving of the Law, Israel's sin with the Golden Calf, the crossing of Jordan, the ascent into the Promised Land. At this point Solomon's bed in Song of Songs 3:7 is taken to be the Temple that he built. The dedication of the Temple follows, and the opening words of chapter 4 of the Song, celebrating the fairness of the bride, are turned into God's acceptance of the sacrifices offered – the lips of verse 3 become the lips of the high priest uttering prayers on the Day of Atonement. This focus on worship is interesting – is it any wonder that Akiba could call the Song 'the Holy of Holies'?

The history proceeds: Israel sins, God leads them into exile, the prophets are sent to wake them from sleep ... To cut a long story short, the climax is the future coming of Messiah and the Messianic Banquet. Let me just share one more quotation to show how the imagery of the Song conveys the thrust of history:

> During the time that the Lord of the world makes His presence to dwell in my midst, I am like the narcissus, fresh from the Garden of Eden and my actions are comely like the rose ... But when I turn from the path which is straight before me, and He removes His Holy Presence from me, I am like the rose that blooms among thorns which pierce and tear her petals, even as I am pierced and torn by the evil decrees in the exile among the nations.

From this you can see that the Targum is in a sense allegorical. But generally speaking it is not like the Gospel interpretation of the parable of the sower, de-coding verbal symbols, each detail corresponding to some other detail. In Jewish tradition, besides the Targum quoted, it seems there is one reading after another that traces out, in a variety of ways, the tempestuous ups and downs of a passionate, stormy relationship, using the lovers' frantic verses of invitation, loss and search, celebration, abandonment and return as a metaphor for the story of another relationship – that of God and his people. The bride is chosen, prized above any other, yet desperately searching, trying to possess; the husband is wild with frustration and longing, anger and joy, as his loved one misbehaves – desire frustrated and fulfilled.

Origen's exegesis of the Song[5]

The Targum itself post-dates the earliest Christian interpretation, but Akiba proves that the tradition goes back much earlier. It would be surprising if there were no influence on the earliest Christian interpretation of the Song of Songs that we now have access to, namely that of Origen in the third century. For it is clear that Origen had scholarly links with contemporary Jews – indeed, he even learned some Hebrew. Origen's *Commentary on the Song of Songs* only survives in an edited Latin translation – Origenism became highly controversial in the centuries after his lifetime and much of his work was lost or modified as a result. But this commentary began a tradition which was taken up by later commentators, such as Gregory of Nyssa and Theodoret; so we can regard it as fairly typical of the patristic approach.

Origen exploits Gospel parables and other biblical texts to identify the bridegroom as Christ and the bride as the Church – we should remember that the fulfilment of the new covenant in Christ meant the Church could be regarded as a 'new Israel'. Origen does not trace history in the Song, like the Jewish exegetes, but rather focuses on the wisdom and understanding that comes to the Church through Christ, her bridegroom. The 'breast' or 'bosom' means the heart, and in the ancient world that meant the mind. Psalm 104:15 speaks of wine to gladden the human heart, and Origen interprets that as a description of the bridegroom's mind – that is, the teachings within him. So when the Song says, 'Your love is better than wine', Origen feels able to comment: 'The Bridegroom's breasts are good because treasures of wisdom and knowledge are concealed in them.' The bride received the Law and the Prophets before the Bridegroom came, but now is amazed and marvelling at the Bridegroom's teachings which combine both old and new. So he moves to the turning of water into wine at Cana, and other Gospel material about new wine reinforces the reading. So the fulfilment in Christ brings wisdom to the Church. Yet the final sentences of this passage in the commentary[6] make the text refer to the progress of the soul from being a child to receiving maturity through the treasures of wisdom and knowledge hidden in the word of God. So Origen oscillates between the Church and the individual soul, implying the same human experience in its individual and corporate aspects. I would contest the widespread view that Origen lays side by side two different interpretations, the ecclesial one and the individualistic one. The close inter-relation between the two is particularly evident when Origen identifies the bed shared by bride and bridegroom as the soul's body, but then observes that our bodies are members of Christ's body and Christ's body is the Church.[7]

In the Prologue to his commentary, Origen relates the three books of Solomon in the biblical canon to three branches of learning. Thus, Proverbs teaches ethics; Ecclesiastes teaches physics; and the Song teaches what he calls 'enoptics', by which he seems to mean insight into the higher realities behind the physical world. The link between Proverbs and ethics makes sense, but that between Ecclesiastes and physics seems to demand some explanation. For Origen 'physics' concerns 'physical things' contrasted with the spiritual, and the big lesson of Ecclesiastes is that 'all is vanity'. It is this which leads one on to the Song and to deeper insight into reality. It is also interesting to note (though the point is not developed by Origen here) that wisdom and foolishness are personified in Proverbs as two women, with strong exhortation not to chase after the harlot. In the Song we find the fulfilment of Wisdom's call.

What Origen is at pains to do, is to sublimate the love expressed in the Song, insisting it is not to be understood in any sort of carnal or fleshly way. He makes a distinction between the inner and the outer self: as the outer self may be moved by earthly desire and love, so the soul is moved by heavenly love and longing when, having clearly beheld the beauty and fairness of the Word of God, it falls deeply in love with his loveliness and receives from the Word himself a certain dart and wound of love.[8]

Song 2:5 reads, 'I have been wounded by love', so it provokes association with Eros or Cupid with his bow and arrows; later Origen will use these phrases: 'the sweet wound of him who is the chosen dart' and 'pierced with the love-worthy spear of his knowledge'.[9] Origen clearly believed that we human beings are all driven by love of something – money or ambition, or pros-titutes, or sporting prowess. So the issue is the directing of that love towards God and neighbour. Being absorbed in passionate devotion of some kind shapes behaviour. So the discourse of passion found in the Song is appropriate for expressing

> this love with which the blessed soul is kindled and inflamed towards the Word of God; [scripture] sings by the Spirit the song of the marriage whereby the Church is joined and allied to Christ the heavenly Bridegroom, desiring to be united to Him through the Word, so that she may conceive by Him and be saved through this chaste begetting of children, when they, conceived as they are by the seed of the Word of God, and born and brought forth by the spotless Church ... shall have persevered in faith and holiness with sobriety (cf. 1 Tim. 2:15).[10]

The Church then produces spiritual children through her mar-riage with Christ, the children then being joined in mystical marriage with the Word of God. The Bride is the Church, and her children are the souls of the faithful; but notice the potential verbal parallels with the conception of Christ by the Holy Spirit of the Virgin Mary, and also the gender reversal which is assisted by the fact that the Greek word for soul (*psyche*) is feminine. We shall return to these observations later.

But now we conclude our exploration of Origen by noting again desire both fulfilled and frustrated, because:

> If there is anyone anywhere who has at some time burned with this faithful love of the Word of God ... so that he yearns and longs for Him day and night, can speak of nothing else by Him, would hear of nothing else but Him, can think of nothing else but Him, and is disposed to no desire or longing nor yet hope, except for Him alone – if such there be, that soul then says in truth, 'I have been wounded by love' (Song 2:5).[11]

We may think back to Jacob disabled by the wound in his thigh. A biblical spirituality is never achieved, never self-satisfied, never comfortable, always longing ... yet always in the Christian tradition, it is also grace received, the fulfilment of promises, the acceptance of Christ. Charles Wesley's hymn expresses the sense of being both at peace and aware of continuing need, longing for more – desire frustrated and fulfilled.

2. Nature and spirituality

We now take a turn in an unexpected direction, and make an apparently unrelated digression. However, our project, you remember, was not just to take over the approach of the Fathers, but also to develop their approach for our own time. Later we will come back to the themes already highlighted.

It is characteristic of love-songs in general and the Song of Songs in particular to use imagery from nature:

> Arise, my darling,
> My fair one, come.
> For, lo, the winter is past.
> The rain is over, gone.
> Blossoms appear in the land,

Pruning-time has come.
The voice of the turtle-dove
Is heard in our land.
The fig ripens her fruits,
The vines in bloom give scent.
Arise, come, my darling,
My fair one, come away. (Song 2:10–13)[12]

The loved one is a dove that hides in the clefts of rock in the cliff, as well as a rose of Sharon, a lily of the valleys, an apple-tree, a gazelle, a young stag, a palm-tree. To describe the physical beauty of the beloved face, eyes, teeth, hair, lips, cheeks and neck, breasts, arms, thighs, belly, head, nose, breath, and so on, the poet uses comparisons with doves, goats, ewes, pomegranates, fawns of a gazelle, springs of water, cedars of Lebanon, wheat, apples. The natural world is celebrated in the language of loving appreciation of the loved one. Yet recall Origen's move from physics to metaphysics ('enoptics', as he called it): Ecclesiastes' 'vanity of vanities, all is vanity' points for him to the inadequacy of the created natural world and the need to move on to insight into the higher realities behind it. Our views of the physical world seem very different. Maybe we need to re-visit the role of creation in a biblical spirituality, especially in this age of ecological concern, as well as greater freedom with respect to our bodily existence and sexual identity.

Besides, is it not true that, especially since the Romantic movement and the poetry of people like Wordsworth, nature has inspired spirituality? People have claimed that it is not in Church but out by the sea, or on the mountains, where they have found God. This, rather than the sublimated eroticism we found in the Fathers, has been more important for spirituality and it has shaped our hymns too. Maybe it is significant that most of the following come from the nineteenth century:

All things bright and beautiful . . .

All things praise thee, Lord most high . . .

For the beauty of the earth . . .

O Lord of heaven and earth and sky . . .

All creatures of our God and King . . .

though the last was, of course, inspired by St Francis, and others
too come from an earlier date:

The spacious firmament on high . . .
(Addison, early eighteenth century)

I sing the Almighty power of God that made the mountains
rise . . .
(and many others by Isaac Watts, also of the early eighteenth
century)

But the point is made: creation inspires worship of the Creator.

In another hymn we find the phrase: 'There is a book who
runs may read' (Keble) – the book turns out to be the Book of
Nature. At a seminar of Muslim and Christian scholars in which I
was involved, there emerged one significant area of agreement –
there are two books, scripture and nature, both of which reveal
God. If we are to love God, then we need both ways of knowing
who it is we love. The message of the book of Job is that we
should not love God for what we get out of it – self-interested
love is not real love. We should love God for God's sake. But the
thrust of God's speech to Job when he eventually confronts him
is that we should also love nature for nature's sake,[13] however
terrifying. This reminds me of a picture I used to contemplate
when meeting in a friend's front room: David Shepherd's
representation of an elephant, face on to the viewer – I always
found it deeply awe-inspiring! It calls us back to the experience
which I had in Botswana,[14] and in particular, to the discovery
that you do not question the elephant's right to charge or the
lion's right to pounce on its prey.

In recent theological literature responding to the ecological
crisis, there has been a critique of the Protestant reading of
Genesis. Exploitation of the earth's resources was justified by the

King James Bible, which translated the Hebrew of Genesis 1:26, 28 to suggest that humankind was to 'have dominion over' nature. The Hebrew, however, should really be translated as 'shepherd'; it is coherent with the image of tending the garden that is found in the following chapter (2:15). It seems to me to be very important in the present context to reclaim the biblical perspective on ourselves as part of creation:

> The fate of humans and the fate of animals is the same; as one dies, so dies the other. They all have the same breath and humans have no advantage over the animals ... All go to one place, all are from the dust and all turn to dust again. Who knows if the human spirit goes upward and the spirit of animals downward to the earth? (Eccles. 3:19)

It is a pity that that passage got forgotten in the great nineteenth-century controversy over Darwin!

In fact, we might also learn from a return to the Fathers about a proper Christian spirituality of the natural world. They were clear that creation is to be appreciated because it is the work of the Creator. The Fathers lived close to the ancient struggle with nature religions, with idolatry, with temple prostitution, with sacred groves of trees embodying the sacralisation of nature. We may well feel it was a scandal that fanatical monks cut down such sacred groves,[15] yet they were making rather too literally a very important theological point. It is one we may need to reclaim in the face of the resurgent paganism of our own time, which is part of a general reaction against Christianity in our culture. The point is set out clearly by Basil of Caesarea.

Basil composed a sequence of nine homilies on the 'Six Days of Creation' (the *Hexaemeron*).[16] He sets out his overall perspective in the first homily. The philosophers (that is, the scientists of his day) have many theories, but their fundamental failing is that they do not recognise that the natural order is God's creation. As he goes through the text of Genesis he adopts much of the scientific knowledge of his own time concerning the natural world, but always to celebrate the wonder of nature and to draw out the ways in which the natural world points beyond itself to its Creator. Doxology, or praise, is the right response. One important aspect of this is the demystification of nature, which he affirms as created 'out of nothing' – it has no inherent divinity. It has been remarked that it was this doctrine which allowed science to develop within Christian culture. Yet the doctrine also hints at a fundamental point for a Christian spirituality of nature – the possibility of rising through contemplation of the created order to knowledge and love of God.

From our earlier explorations[17] you may recall that the Cappadocian Fathers made it very clear that you cannot know God's essence, though you can know the divine 'energies' or 'activities'. Creation is one source of that knowledge. The important thing is that nature points beyond itself, like the text of Scripture, and also like our own physicality. For we ourselves are part of the natural order – bodily creatures – and the sexuality of the Song of Songs is a feature that might again lead us to go beyond Origen and his successors, who tended to be enamoured by virginity (or more correctly, celibacy). Origen was concerned about carnality, but feminist theology, in particular, has turned to the Song of Songs for a celebration of woman and body. We seem less happy than previous generations with treating our bodies as mere containers for the immortal soul, recognising that we express our personalities physically, we relate to one another physically, we are psychosomatic wholes. We know we belong to the natural order as naked apes, even though we may have some exceptionally developed faculties, like language and rationality; but even these gifts are simply more sophisticated versions of what is found in animals and birds.

Perhaps surprisingly, deeper exploration of the Fathers proves that in the fourth century they too were aware of the intimate relationship between soul and body, and of our place within the created order. Parallels between the bodily senses and the senses of the spirit were what made possible their treatment of the Song of Songs as a devotional text, and they also imply affirmation of the bodily, despite the appearance of suspicion of everything

Brokenness and Blessing

carnal. Gregory of Nyssa wrote a work on the 'Making of Man' (*De Opificio Hominis*)[18] – it was a continuation of his brother Basil's *Hexaemeron*. He gave an account of the relationship of the soul and body which reads as if the soul is roughly equivalent to what we would call the central nervous system, and he was not the only one – we can compare the work on the 'Nature of Man' (*De Natura Hominis*)[19] by Nemesius, a near contemporary.[20] Both Gregory in the East and Augustine in the West, against the tendencies of the Neo-platonists by whom both were influenced, argued for the resurrection of the body. They looked forward to the transformation of embodied life, recognising that there could be no full-bodied living without some kind of physical expression of our being and relationships.

Yet the experience of being physical beings lies at the very cusp of the ambiguity of our human condition. Vulnerability, corruptibility, mortality are characteristic of the physical, natural world – 'Change and decay in all around I see'! The Fathers were highly sensitive to this reality, but they saw this mortal, natural existence, with all its passions and joys, pointing beyond itself to that full-bodied living which is God's ultimate purpose. The physical senses are analogous to the spiritual; physical love is stimulated by beauty, and the beauty of God evokes spiritual love: 'My God, how wonderful Thou art!' For the Fathers, 'anagogy' meant the spiritual journey upwards through analogy. It counter-balanced their apophaticism.

So we are called to love of nature for nature's sake, as to love of neighbour for the neighbour's sake, of the stranger for the stranger's sake, of our enemy for the enemy's sake, not our own, but all alike are subsumed in love of God for God's sake. They are the outcome of the overspill of God's love filling us to overflowing. When a lover sings a love-song, it is sheer admiration and praise for the loved one; the singer is transported beyond the singer's self, otherwise love is corrupted into self-interest, possessiveness, jealousy … So let's return to the Song and the question of loving God, as we draw together these reflections on biblical spirituality.

3. How are we to love God whom we have not seen?

According to 1 John, we love God whom we have not seen by loving the brother whom we have seen. Certainly that is an expression of our love for God, and another appropriate stepping-stone ('anagogy') for love of God. But how are we to kindle the passionate response of 'My God, how wonderful Thou art!'? Our ascent (*anabasis*) depends on Christ's descent (*katabasis*). Like 1 John, the Fathers were clear that God first loved us: 'In this is love, not that we loved God, but that he loved us and sent his Son . . .' The movement explored in our third chapter is central to a Christian biblical spirituality.

Gregory of Nyssa

For Gregory, the response to this love is supremely expressed in the Song. The key feature of the Christian soul is receptivity to God, like that of Mary. I am indebted to Verna Harrison for illuminating these issues:[21] as Mary's 'purity and integrity open[ed] a place within her where God [could] enter, where Christ [could] be formed . . .', so the soul 'receives the entrance of God and brings forth Christ, though spiritually, not physically'. Mary's receptivity is intrinsic to her creaturehood – she lives by participation in God, like all human persons. God is bridegroom and Mary's motherhood typifies that of every believer. In Salisbury Cathedral Close is a remarkable statue of Mary, now old, long after the events of her Son's death and resurrection, 'striding forth to bring Christ into the world': the 'Walking Madonna' is a 'type' of the Christian life.

According to Verna Harrison, for Gregory, Proverbs represents the immature soul, receiving instruction from its parents, like a youth entranced with Wisdom's beauty, or conversely tempted by the harlot, by foolishness. Proverbs 31 depicts the soul's marriage with one whom Gregory describes as a 'manly woman', Wisdom as Christ. This leads to Ecclesiastes, which teaches the soul to abandon external things, which are transitory

Brokenness and Blessing

and vain, and prepares the way for the Song of Songs. Now roles are reversed – the soul becomes the bride, the woman, by 'typical patristic gender bending'. The soul is the 'receptacle' of God, the Bridegroom, experiencing always an insatiable longing for the Infinite:

> The soul seeking God must reach outward beyond the boundary of her own capacity into the incomprehensible. In this situation, the young man's quest for acquisition, possession and control of Wisdom can only be abandoned.

Instead there can only be grateful reception of grace.

The language of desire and longing expresses for Gregory the eternal *epektasis*, reaching out and striving forward, never fully attained ... For no created being can ever grasp the infinite Being of God, who is in principle beyond our grasp, incomprehensible – otherwise God would be reduced to the size of a created mind. We recall earlier chapters: God is beyond us; our presumption is crippled in struggling with God. Yet it is this wound of love which is our salvation. For Gregory the goal is not to suppress passion but to redirect it to the appropriate object:

> When the [soul] has torn herself from her attachment to sin, and by that mystic kiss she yearns to bring her mouth close to the fountain of light, then does she become beautiful, radiant with the light of truth, having washed away the dark stain of ignorance.[22]

Gregory believes there is a correspondence between the motions and movements of the soul and the sense organs of the body; so our earthly response to beauty gives us a taste of what it would mean to transcend surface appearance and discern the Lord as the object of beauty *par excellence*. As for Origen the arrow of love wounds us:

> From the scriptures we learn that God is love and also that he sends forth His only-begotten Son as his 'chosen arrow' (Isaiah 49:20) to the elect, dipping the triple point at its tip in the Spirit

of life ... It is a good wound and a sweet point by which life penetrates the soul; for by the tearing of the arrow she opens a kind of door, an entrance into herself. For no sooner does she receive the dart of love, than the image of archery is transformed into a scene of nuptial joy.[23]

For Gregory, then, the love of God requires receptivity, the abandonment of the desire to possess and control, and the acceptance of an eternal longing that can never be satisfied, a wounding with love's arrow that brings fulfilment as well as frustration. In these graphic images he expresses the apophatic, the anagogic and the katabatic moves involved in knowledge and love of God: one has to hold together (1) the denial of likeness to anything created and so the confession of God's absolute transcendence, (2) the movement upwards from created things to a mind-blowing perception of higher reality, and (3) reception from the downward act of God's revelatory accommodation to the human level in the language of Scripture and the life of Christ.

Augustine

Gregory's picture is mirrored in the thinking of Augustine, for whom prayer is always a yearning, a desire, the heart's longing for God, as the Christian lives the life of a pilgrim, progressing towards eternal happiness, to the enjoyment of God for God's sake.[24] Scripture provides a language in which to express this inner longing – for in yearning for God, the petitioner yearns for what exceeds human understanding. So progress involves learning ignorance. Yet one needs some knowledge of the object of one's desire in order to desire it, and that is the gift of the Holy Spirit.

So even in this life on earth the joyous heart may praise God, in words and songs, on musical instruments, though ultimately praise will be jubilation beyond words. Meanwhile, desire, like fire, needs stoking if it is not to die; so a discipline of prayer is needed. Furthermore, there needs to be a congruence between

Brokenness and Blessing

the external words of Scripture, its preaching and the prayers of the Church, and the internal yearning of the heart. That congruence comes from the Holy Spirit. And because we are made in God's image, the yearning that reaches out to God is a return to oneself. Time and again Augustine discusses the difference between enjoying and using, by which he implies exploiting – this seems to be the parallel to Gregory's rejection of possession. Love of God must be for God's sake. The intermittent alleluias of our pilgrimage express the desire for the eternal alleluia; our hearts are restless till they find their rest in God. The desire that God gives, God also satisfies, while at the same time increasing desire and capacity for reception. Knowledge grows as love grows.

4. The outskirts of God's ways and our transformation

So the Song of Songs is the Holy of Holies, because God does not dwell in temples made with hands (Acts 7:48). Christianity was a mighty revolution – all religious architecture in the ancient world provided palaces for the gods, and the people stayed outside. When we visited the temples in Egypt we discovered, deep inside, scratched Christian symbols – Christians invaded the temples, and this was not just a challenge to idolatry, but to the whole tradition of locating the divine on earth. The divine presence was to be found, not in sacred temples and images, but in human beings, in saints, gathered as the body of Christ on earth and as temples of the Holy Spirit. This divine presence was mediated through the incarnation and so through Mary, *Theotokos* – Mother of God.

In his exposition Augustine treats Psalm 42[25] as essentially about contemplation: 'As the hart pants for the water-brooks, so my soul pants for Thee, O God'. Verse 4 speaks of going to the place of the wonderful tabernacle, the house of God, with the voice of joy and praise, the sound of feasting. Augustine speaks of blundering about outside the tabernacle seeking God, but then entering and wondering at the things inside. He suggests that human beings are the tabernacle of God on earth, to be admired for their discipline, their service to God in good works and their obedience to God who transforms their desires from inside. The psalmist, he says, gazes at the same virtues in his own soul and crosses deeper into the sanctuary to find wisdom's water-fountain, and following on a certain sweetness, some inner and hidden delight, he is led on, hearing a kind of interior music, celebrating a festival, sounds of joy and praise. So a psalm about going to the Jerusalem Temple becomes a celebration of the Church and of the contemplation of the soul, the outer and the inner of Christian devotion. The Song of Songs is the Holy of Holies because it teases the heart into love of God, into a yearning fulfilled yet ever frustrated. Maybe we find something like this experience more easily by listening to the slow move-ment of Mozart's *Clarinet Quintet*, with its expression of the yearning and longing inseparable from peace, joy, beauty; maybe we do not so naturally associate it with Church or reading Scripture. But this is why, traditionally, people have spoken of 'Christian devotion'.

So we return to where we began in the first chapter. Gregory of Nyssa and others were fascinated by John 1:18: 'No one has ever seen God. It is God the only Son who is in the bosom of the Father, who has made him known.' Famously Moses had asked to see God: 'Show me your glory, I pray' (Exod. 33:18). God replied:

> I will make all my goodness pass before you ... But ... you cannot see my face, for no one shall see me and live [an idea found in many other places in the Bible]. See, there is a place by me where you shall stand on the rock; and while my glory passes by I will put you in a cleft of the rock, and I will cover you with my hand until I have passed by; then I will take away my hand, and you shall see my back; but my face shall not be seen. (Exod. 33:19–20)

Yet earlier in the chapter we read, 'Thus the Lord used to speak with Moses face to face as one speaks to a friend' (v. 11); and in the next chapter we find Moses' face shining because he had been talking with God (34:29) ... God's elusiveness, yet God's grace and presence, strangely belong together. We see only the out-skirts of God's ways, in creation, in Scripture, in the saints, in the poor and the stranger, in the ordinariness of life, which has its sacramental dimension as it points beyond itself. Yet in the incarnation God accommodates the divine self to us, talks with us as a friend ('I do not call you servants any longer ... but I have called you friends' – John 15:15), and washes our feet.

If you go on a trip to the Mendips you may be shown the 'Rock of Ages', where Toplady sheltered from a storm and was inspired to write the hymn, 'Rock of Ages cleft for me'. I ask myself, Is this story a literalising myth? What about the biblical resonances? Moses is hidden in the cleft of a rock while God passes by. Elijah runs away into the desert, and there is a terrible storm – electrifying and energising, terrible and lovely as storms can be – yet he discovers that God is not in the storm but in a still, small voice (or as the NRSV puts it, 'sheer silence' – 1 Kings 19). And the cleft in the rock becomes Christ's riven side where we can shelter from the terror of God's passing, like Moses – for no one can see God face to face and live.

Desire frustrated and fulfilled ... One of the implicit points of this exploration of a biblical spirituality has been that our hym-nography is nearer to a truly traditional reading of the Bible, indeed a reading in continuity with the Fathers, than modernist, historico-critical readings. So the climax of this chapter can only be the most well known of all Charles Wesley's hymns:

Love divine, all loves excelling,
Joy of heaven to earth come down,
Fix is us thy humble dwelling,
All thy faithful mercies crown.
Jesu, thou art all compassion,
Pure, unbounded love thou art;
Visit us with thy salvation,
Enter every trembling heart.

Come, almighty to deliver,
Let us all thy life receive;
Suddenly return, and never,
Never more thy temples leave.
Thee we would be always
  blessing,
Serve thee as thy hosts above,
Pray, and praise thee, without
  ceasing,
Glory in thy perfect love.

Finish then thy new creation,
Pure and spotless let us be;
Let us see thy great salvation,
Perfectly restored in thee:
Changed from glory into glory,
Till in heaven we take our place,
Till we cast our crowns before thee,
Lost in wonder, love and praise!

CONCLUSION

We have been on a journey together, a slightly longer one than was possible when the lectures were delivered, as I have taken the opportunity to fill out some of the stages a little more fully. But looking back, it is possible to see how the five stages in the journey complement one another, and how, as they do so, they challenge some current assumptions about the world and about Christianity's understanding of it. We are asked to leave our comfort zones, to stem our anxieties about suffering and death, and to cease assuming that self-fulfilment is the goal of spirituality; and yet the outcome of the pilgrimage will undoubtedly be the discovery of ourselves in a new dimension.

The wilderness is not a comfortable place to be, but it is a place where one is more likely to meet God and discover one's own limitations. Peace is hardly found when wrestling with God, and one can end up wounded and disabled; yet the wound of love is exactly what heals us. The way of Jesus involves self-emptying, and it is when we can allow the 'other', the stranger, those who are different, to challenge our self-sufficiency that we learn what it means to be his disciples. So a biblical spirituality necessitates openness, receptivity and mutuality, not patronising 'do-gooding' backed up by the assurance that we are right and we have power because we are sent by God.

Disability is the condition of blessing. Humankind has overreached itself, forgotten its essential creatureliness and its role in creation's ecology, and put itself in God's place. The rediscovery that God is beyond us, yet reaches out in Christ to grasp our hands in the midst of the struggle, even to wound us with his arrow of love, might enable us, both individually and as the body of Christ on earth, to live the way of love and true humility in following Jesus. And maybe this would make us the best witnesses to the Gospel in the pluralist global village of the twenty-first century.

Frances Young
August 2006

BIBLIOGRAPHY

Primary sources

For the benefit of a more general readership I have listed only English versions, apart from cases where no translation exists. Where possible I have referred to Penguin translations or volumes of *The Classics of Western Spirituality* (= *CWS*, published New York: the Paulist Press). Otherwise I cite the volumes of the *Library of Christian Classics* (= *LCC*, published London: SCM Press), the *Ancient Christian Writers* series (= *ACW*, published New York: the Newman Press), the *Fathers of the Church* series (= *FC*, published Washington, DC: the Catholic University of America Press) or the nineteenth-century volumes of the *Ante-Nicene Christian Library* (= *ANCL*), the *Ante-Nicene Fathers* (= *ANF*, reissued Grand Rapids: Eerdmans) or the *Nicene and Post-Nicene Fathers* (= *NPNF*, reissued Grand Rapids: Eerdmans). These series should be easily available in theological libraries.

Ambrose, *On Duties*, ET *NPNF*
—, *Seven Exegetical Sermons*, ET *FC* vol. 65
Apophthegmata Patrum, in Helen Waddell, *The Desert Fathers*, London: Collins-Fontana, 1965 (first published by Constable, 1936)
Apostolic Constitutions, ET *ANF*
Apostolic Fathers, ET Penguin, *FC* vol. 1, or *LCC*
Athanasius, *Life of Antony*, ET *CWS*
Augustine, *City of God*, ET Penguin or *FC* vols. 8 & 14
—, *Enarrationes in Psalmos* (*Explanations of the Psalms*), ET *ACW*
—, *On Christian Teaching*, ET by R. P. H. Green in Oxford World's Classics, Oxford: OUP 1997
Basil of Caesarea, *Hexaemeron*, ET *NPNF*
Clement of Alexandria, *Paedagogus*, ET *FC* vol. 23, or *ANCL*
Cyril of Alexandria, *On Worship in Spirit and in Truth*, Greek text in Migne, *PG* 68; no ET available. ET of selections of his works in Norman Russell (ed.), *Cyril of Alexandria* in *The Early Church Fathers* series, London: Routledge 2000.
Cyril of Jerusalem, *Catechetical Orations*, ET *FC* vol. 61
—, ET of selections of his work in Edward Yarnold, SJ (ed.), *Cyril of Jerusalem* in *The Early Church Fathers* series, London: Routledge 2000

Ephrem the Syrian, *Hymns on Paradise*, Introduction and ET by Sebastian Brock, New York: St Vladimir's Seminary Press, 1990

—, extracts in Sebastian Brock, *The Luminous Eye*, Rome: CIIS 1985

Epistle to Diognetus, see *Apostolic Fathers*

Eusebius of Caesarea, *Ecclesiastical History*, ET Penguin or *FC* vol. 29

—, *Preparation for the Gospel*, text, ET and notes by E. H. Gifford, Oxford: OUP 1903

Gregory of Nazianzus, ET in F. W. Norris *et al.*, *Faith gives Fullness to Reasoning: The Five Theological Orations of Gregory of Nazianzus*, introduction and commentary F. W. Norris, ET L. Wickham and F. Williams, Leiden: Brill, 1991; or *NPNF*

Gregory of Nyssa, *Life of Moses*, ET in *CWS*

—, see also *From Glory to Glory. Texts from Gregory of Nyssa's mystical writings*, trans. & ed. Herbert Musurillo, with an introduction by Jean Daniélou, New York: Scribner's 1961

—, *De Opificio Hominis* (*On the Making of Man*), ET in *NPNF*

Hilary of Poitiers, *On the Trinity*, ET *FC* vol. 25

—, *On the Synods*, ET *NPNF*

Ignatius, see *Apostolic Fathers*

Irenaeus, *Against the Heresies*, ET in *ANCL*

—, *The Demonstration of the Apostolic Preaching*, ET by John Behr, Crestwood, NY: St Vladimir's Seminary Press 1997, or by J. A. Robinson, London: SPCK 1920

—, ET of selections of his works in R. M. Grant (ed.), *Irenaeus of Lyons* in *The Early Church Fathers* series, London: Routledge 2000

Jerome, *Against the Pelagians*, ET *FC* vol. 53

—, *Epistles*, ET *NPNF*

John Chrysostom, *Homilies on Genesis*, Greek text in Migne, *PG* 53–4

—, ET of selections of his work in *FC* vols. 33, 41, 68 & 72, and *NPNF* Series I vols. IX–XIV

Justin Martyr, *I & II Apology*, ET *FC* vol. 6 and *ANCL*

—, *Dialogue with Trypho*, ET *FC* vol. 6 and *ANCL*

Leo the Great, *Epistles*, ET *NPNF*

Macarian Homilies, ET in *Pseudo-Macarius, The Fifty Spiritual Homilies and the Great Letter*, *CWS*

—, see also John Wesley's *Christian Library*, vol. 1

Nemesius, *On the Nature of Man*, ET in *LCC*

Origen, *On First Principles*, ET G. W. Butterworth, London: SPCK 1936; reissued Gloucester, Mass.: Peter Smith 1973

—, *Against Celsus*, ET Henry Chadwick, Cambridge: CUP 1965

—, *Commentary on John*, ET Ronald Heine, *FC* vols. 80 & 89

—, *On the Song of Songs*, ET R. P. Lawson, *ACW*

Secondary sources

Aulen, Gustaf, *Christus Victor*, ET by A. G. Hebert, London: SPCK 1931

Brook, Peter, *The Empty Space*, London: MacGibbon & Kee 1968

Burton-Christie, Douglas, *The Word in the Desert. Scripture and the Quest for Holiness in Early Christian Monasticism*, New York and Oxford: OUP 1993

Camus, Albert, *The Outsider*, ET Penguin Classics 1982 (first published in French 1942)

Carruthers, Mary, *The Craft of Thought*, Cambridge: CUP 1998

Chitty, Derwas J., *The Desert a City. An Introduction to the Study of Egyptian and Palestinian Monasticism under the Christian Empire*, London and Oxford: Mowbrays 1966

Clark, Elizabeth, *Reading Renunciation: Asceticism and Scripture in Early Christianity*, Princeton: Princeton University Press 1999

Cohen, Ian, 'They endure all disabilities as aliens' in *Mental Handicap, Theology and Pastoral Care*, ed. Stephen Pattison, University of Birmingham 1986

Davidson, Robert, *Genesis 12—50*, Cambridge: CUP 1979

Douglas, Mary, *Purity and Danger*, London: Routledge & Kegan Paul 1966

Etty, *The Letters and Diaries of Etty Hillesum 1941–1943*, ed. Klaas A. D. Smelik, trans. Arnold J. Pomerans, Grand Rapids: Eerdmans and Ottawa: Novalis 2002

Frend, W. H. C., *Martyrdom and Persecution in the Early Church*, Oxford: Blackwell 1965

Grant, R. M., *The Earliest Lives of Jesus*, London 1961

Harrison, Verna, 'Gender, Generation and Virginity in Cappadocian Theology', *Journal of Theological Studies* NS 47 (1996), pp. 38–68

Hauerwas, Stanley and William H. Willimon, *Resident Aliens: Life in the Christian Colony. A provocative Christian assessment of culture and ministry for people who know something is wrong*, Nashville: Abingdon Press 1990

Hick, John (ed.), *The Myth of God Incarnate*, London: SCM 1977

Inge, John, *A Christian Theology of Place*, Aldershot: Ashgate 2003

Lane, Belden C., *The Solace of Fierce Landscapes. Exploring Desert and Mountain Spirituality*, New York and Oxford: OUP 1998

Lane Fox, Robin, *Pagans and Christians*, London: Penguin 1986

Louth, Andrew, *The Wilderness of God*, London: DLT 1991

Malone, E. E., *The Monk and the Martyr*, Washington, DC: Catholic University of America 1950

McDannell, Colleen and Bernhard Lang, *Heaven. A History*, New Haven: Yale University Press, 1990

Merton, Thomas, *Elected Silence*, London: Hollis and Carter 1949 (English edition of *The Seven Storey Mountain*)

Mitchell, Margaret M. and Frances M. Young (eds), *The Cambridge History of Christianity: Origins to Constantine*, Cambridge: CUP 2006

Nussbaum, Martha, *The fragility of goodness*, Cambridge: CUP 1986

Pope, Marvin H., *Commentary on the Song of Songs*, in the Anchor Bible series, New York: Doubleday 1977

Turner, Denys, *The Darkness of God*, Cambridge: CUP 1995

—, *Faith Seeking*, London: SCM Press 2002

Vanier, Jean, *Finding Peace*, London: Continuum 2003

—, *The Broken Body*, London: DLT 1988.

Von Rad, Gerhard, *Genesis*, ET John H. Marks, revised ed. London: SCM 1972

Wakefield, Gordon (ed.), *A Dictionary of Christian Spirituality*, London: SCM Press 1983

Weaver, Rebecca H., 'Prayer' in *Augustine through the Ages. An Encyclopedia*, ed. Allan D. Fitzgerald OSA, Eerdmans 1999

Weil, Simone, *Gateway to God*, selected works ed. David Raper, London: Fontana 1974

Westermann, C., *Genesis 12—36*, ET John J. Scullion SJ, London: SPCK 1985

Williams, Rowan, *The Wound of Knowledge*, London: DLT 1990 (2nd edn)

Young, Frances, Lewis Ayres and Andrew Louth (eds), *The Cambridge History of Early Christian Literature*, Cambridge: CUP 2004

Young, Frances, *The Art of Performance*, London: DLT 1990

—, *Face to Face. A Narrative Essay in the theology of Suffering*, Edinburgh: T. & T. Clark 1990

— (ed.), *Encounter with Mystery. Reflections on L'Arche and Living with Disability*, London: DLT 1997

—, *Biblical Exegesis and the Formation of Christian Culture*, Cambridge: CUP 1997

—, 'Adam, the Soul and Immortality: A Study of the Interaction of "Science" and the Bible in some Anthropological Treatises of the Fourth Century', in *Vigiliae Christianae* 37 (1983), pp. 110–40

—, 'The Mark of the Nails', in Stephen Barton and Graham Stanton (eds), *Resurrection: Essays in Honour of Leslie Houlden*, London: SPCK 1994

—, 'Suffering', in Adrian Hastings, Alistair Mason and Hugh Pyper (eds), *The Oxford Companion to Christian Thought*, Oxford: OUP 2000, pp. 687–9

—, '*Creatio ex nihilo*: a context for the emergence of the Christian doctrine of creation', in *Scottish Journal of Theology* 44 (1991), pp. 139–51

—, 'Sexuality and Devotion: Mystical Readings of the Song of Songs' in *Theology and Sexuality* no. 14 (2001), pp. 80–96

—, 'Inner struggle: Some Parallels between John Wesley and the Greek Fathers', in S. T. Kimbrough, Jr (ed.), *Orthodox and Wesleyan Spirituality*, Crestwood, New York: St Vladimir's Seminary Press 2002

—, '*Theotokos*: Mary and the Pattern of Fall and Redemption in the Theology of Cyril of Alexandria', in Thomas G. Weinandy and Daniel A. Keating (eds), *The Theology of St Cyril of Alexandria. A Critical Appreciation*, London: T. & T. Clark 2003

NOTES

Introduction

1. See further *The Cambridge History of Early Christian Literature*.

Chapter 1. THE DESERT EXPERIENCE

1. Derwas Chitty picked up this phrase from the *Life of Antony* 14 as the title of his book on the desert monks.
2. Quoted from Helen Waddell, *The Desert Fathers*, p. 103; from *The Sayings of the Fathers* (translated into Latin by Pelagius the Deacon and John the Subdeacon) VII.33.
3. Gustaf Aulen, *Christus Victor*, classically explored this theme.
4. *Apophthegmata Patrum*: Alphabetic Collection, Theodora 2; quoted from Burton-Christie, *The Word in the Desert* (pp. 198–9), to which this and the following paragraphs are indebted.
5. *Apophthegmata Patrum*: Alphabetic Collection, Antony 3; quoted from Burton-Christie, op. cit. (p. 213).
6. Burton-Christie, op. cit., p. 198.
7. Ibid., p. 152.
8. *Apophthegmata Patrum*: Alphabetic Collection, Macarius the Great 3; quoted from Burton-Christie, op. cit. (p. 125).
9. *Apophthegmata Patrum*: Alphabetic Collection, John the Persian 4; quoted from Burton-Christie, op. cit. (p. 168).
10. *Apophthegmata Patrum*: Alphabetic Collection, Hyperchius 8; quoted from Burton-Christie, op. cit. (p. 243).
11. *Apophthegmata Patrum*: Alphabetic Collection, Nilus 8; quoted from Burton-Christie, op. cit. (p. 241).
12. The following discussion draws from my book, *Biblical Exegesis and the Formation of Christian Culture*, pp. 258–62.
13. *Life of Moses* I.5; *CWS*, p. 30.
14. *Life of Moses* I.16–77; *CWS*, pp. 33–51.
15. *Life of Moses* II.227; *CWS*, pp. 113–14.
16. *Life of Moses* II.192; *CWS*, p. 104.
17. *Life of Moses* II.162ff; *CWS*, pp. 94–6.

18. *Life of Moses* II.217–55; *CWS*, pp. 111–20.
19. *Life of Moses* II.239; *CWS*, p. 116.
20. *Life of Moses* II.252; *CWS*, p. 119.
21. *Against Eunomius* II.84ff.
22. *Commentary on the Song of Songs*, as quoted by Daniélou in Musurillo, *From Glory to Glory*, p. 23.
23. *Life of Moses*, as quoted (slightly altered) by Daniélou in Musurillo, op. cit., p. 29.
24. *Commentary on Ecclesiastes*, cf. *Commentary on the Beatitudes*, both quoted by Daniélou in Musurillo, op. cit., pp. 42–3.
25. *Great Catechesis* 21, quoted by Daniélou in Musurillo, op. cit., p. 48.
26. *Life of Moses*, as quoted by Daniélou in Musurillo, op. cit., p. 48.
27. *On Perfection*, ET in Musurillo, op. cit., pp. 83–4.
28. *Commentary on the Song of Songs*, quoted by Daniélou in Musurillo, op. cit., pp. 68–9.
29. *Life of Moses*, in Musurillo, op. cit., p. 148.
30. The following draws on my chapter, '*Theotokos*: Mary and the Pattern of Fall and Redemption in the Theology of Cyril of Alexandria' in *The Theology of St Cyril of Alexandria*. The work, *On Worship in Spirit and in Truth* is not available in English translation.
31. The quotation is taken from the ET by Sebastian Brock, p. 171.
32. In *The Empty Space*. There he also reflects on 'Holy Theatre' in an interesting way.
33. 'The Mark of the Nails' in Barton and Stanton (eds), *Resurrection*.
34. Cf. Martha Nussbaum, *The fragility of goodness*, p. 37.
35. *Purity and Danger*, pp. 163ff.
36. This point is made explicit by Origen, but underlies the exegetical endeavours of others, such as the Antiochenes and Augustine.
37. For further discussion see my books, *The Art of Performance* and *Biblical Exegesis*.
38. *Encounter with Mystery*, pp. 89–93.
39. *Elected Silence*, p. 139.
40. First published in *Face to Face*, pp. 4–7, slightly altered here in view of developments in politically correct language! Based on the version of the Psalms in the *Alternative Service-Book*.

Chapter 2. WRESTLING JACOB

1. Westermann, *Genesis 12—36*, p. 519; discussion from pp. 516–21.
2. Davidson, *Genesis 12—50*, pp. 183–5.
3. See, e.g., von Rad, *Genesis*, pp. 319ff.
4. Davidson, op. cit., p. 186.
5. Quoted by von Rad, op. cit., p. 326.
6. *Ecclesiastical History* I.2.

Brokenness and Blessing

7. *Dialogue with Trypho* 58.

8. *Catechetical Oration* 12.16.

9. 'On the Trinity iv.31, xii.46; *On the Synods* 49.

10. *Epistle* 31.

11. *Apostolic Constitutions* v.20.

12. *Paedagogus* I.vii.

13. *On First Principles* III.ii.5.

14. *Preparation for the Gospel* IX.6; cf. VII.8.

15. *On the Trinity* v.19–20.

16. *Against the Pelagians* iii.8.

17. *Epistle* 22.11.

18. Elizabeth Clark, *Reading Renunciation*.

19. *Sermon* V.6.

20. *Sermons* IV & V.

21. *City of God* XVI.39; cf. Ambrose, 'Jacob and the Happy Life' II.7.31.

22. 'Jacob and the Happy Life', in *Seven Exegetical Sermons*; see especially II.7.30.

23. Cf. *On Duties* I.120.

24. Ibid.

25. *City of God* XVI.39.

26. This paragraph owes much to my article, 'Suffering', in *The Oxford Companion to Christian Thought*.

27. *Elected Silence*, p. 139.

28. See Chapter 1.

29. This is, of course, a huge generalisation, undermined in fact by my own reference to Thomas Merton: for a corrective see the works of Denys Turner, which explore medieval apophaticism, and on atheism, see his inaugural lecture, published in *Faith Seeking*.

30. This well-known description originated with Harnack, the great liberal scholar of the late nineteenth century.

31. *Faith* 31.6–7, as quoted by Brock, *Luminous Eye*, pp. 43–5.

32. Quoted by Brock, op. cit., p. 38, from a poem attributed to Ephrem.

33. *Faith* 32.9, as quoted by Brock, op. cit., p. 38.

34. *Faith* 6.3, as quoted by Brock, op. cit., p. 38.

35. *Faith* 4.9, as quoted by Brock, op. cit., p. 39.

36. *Faith* 18.6, as quoted by Brock, op. cit., p. 43.

37. For fuller treatment, see my article, 'Creatio ex nihilo'.

38. Quoted from Helen Waddell, *The Desert Fathers*, p. 81; from *The Sayings of the Fathers* (translated into Latin by Pelagius the Deacon and John the Subdeacon) II.2.

39. See my article, 'Inner struggle'.

40. Maloney, *Pseudo-Macarius*, 85.

41. Hom. IV.9, as translated in Wesley, *Christian Library*.

42. Hom. VI.4, as translated in Wesley, *Christian Library*.

1. For my own brief history of the Quest, see the 'Prelude' to *The Cambridge History of Christianity: Origins to Constantine*, pp. 1–34.
2. E.g. Cerinthus; see Irenaeus, *Against the Heresies* I.21.
3. One of the books of the 'Apocrypha', according to the post-Reformation canon of Scripture, but part of the Greek Bible used by the Fathers.
4. *Trallians* ix–x.
5. *Ephesians* xx.2.
6. *Trallians* x.
7. Irenaeus, *Demonstration of the Apostolic Preaching* 32–34; and many other places in his work *Against the Heresies*.
8. *Against the Heresies* V.2.
9. *Demonstration* 11; preface to *Against the Heresies* IV.
10. *I Apology* 66.
11. Eusebius, *Ecclesiastical History* VI.12.
12. See discussion in *The Cambridge History of Christianity: Origins to Constantine*, pp. 2, 7.
13. *I Apology* 30.
14. *I Apology* 32ff.
15. *I Apology* 13–17.
16. *I Apology* 46; *II Apology* 10.
17. Eusebius, *Ecclesiastical History* VII.22.
18. Eusebius, *Ecclesiastical History* VI.42.
19. Origen, *Against Celsus*, particularly I.66–70.
20. For further discussion of the above points in this paragraph, see the 'Prelude' to *The Cambridge History of Christianity: Origins to Constantine*.
21. This text is usually found among the so-called *Apostolic Fathers*.
22. Frend, *Martyrdom and Persecution*, ch. 12.
23. This metaphor is borrowed from Aulen, *Christus Victor*.
24. *Commentary on John* VI.36.
25. A rather broad generalisation, but supported by Malone, *The Monk and the Martyr*.
26. Burton Christie, *The Word in the Desert*, ch. 8.
27. This paragraph is based on the homily found in *NPNF*, 1st series, vol. IX, pp. 199–207. It is typical of a great deal of Chrysostom's preaching, though the volume fails to make clear how the exact source of the Greek original of this homily might be traced.
28. For further discussion see my article, '*Theotokos*: Mary and the Pattern of Fall and Redemption in the Theology of Cyril of Alexandria'.
29. *Commentary on Isaiah* 7.14–16 (Russell, p. 79).
30. *Commentary on John* 17.11 (Russell, pp. 125–6).
31. *Commentary on Isaiah* 11.1–3 (Russell, pp. 83–4).
32. *Commentary on John* 6.35 (Russell, pp. 110–11).
33. 6.53, pp. 115ff.

34. 6.54, pp. 117–18.
35. The furore over *The Myth of God Incarnate* simply confirmed both these points.
36. Public interest in the *Da Vinci Code* illuminates the post-modern mind-set, driven by the desire for fact, indeed to find an authentic version that contests the authoritative tradition, while uncritically allowing fiction to masquerade as fact.
37. *Encounter with Mystery*, p. xi.
38. This story has previously been told in *Face to Face*.

Chapter 4. STRANGERS AND EXILES

1. Augustine, *City of God* XIV.28; all references to this work will in future be given in brackets in the text. The translation cited is that of Henry Bettenson, edited by David Knowles, in the Pelican Classics.
2. Gutierrez, quoted in John Inge, *A Christian Theology of Place*, p. 38.
3. Stanley Hauerwas and William H. Willimon, *Resident Aliens*, pp. 24, 49, 51, 83.
4. The papers were collected and reproduced in a private publication entitled *Mental Handicap, Theology and Pastoral Care*, ed. Stephen Pattison.
5. *Purity and Danger*, p. 35.
6. Ibid., p. 162.
7. Ibid., pp. 163ff.
8. *Encounter with Mystery*, p. xi.
9. In Chronicles, the son of Jonathan is named Meribbaal. This would have meant 'the Lord is Advocate', and was almost certainly the original name. But names containing 'baal' became unmentionable after the long struggle by the prophets to focus Hebrew worship on the one true God rather than the local fertility baals. So rather than write *baal*, the story-teller wrote *bosheth* = 'shame'. So we have the politically incorrect suggestion that 'shame' was the name of a 'cripple'. Of course, having a disability is nothing to be ashamed of, but many human societies have behaved as if it were. So let's face the potential shock: this is the story of Mephibosheth, a person with disabilities, whose name is 'shame'. Once I wrote a verse dialogue based on this story in an attempt to capture these dynamics. It began:

> Shame is my name
> Lame are my feet
> Shunned is my face
> My fame is disgrace.

And it ended with an outburst, for which there's no biblical basis, but which expressed the outrage felt by people with disabilities when all they receive is charity and patronage rather than respect, dignity and equality.
10. Among his writings I refer to *The Broken Body*.

11. Afterword to *The Outsider*, Penguin ET, p. 119.
12. *Finding Peace*, p. 72.
13. *De Doctrina Christiana*, Book I.

Chapter 5. DESIRE FRUSTRATED AND FULFILLED

1. *The Dictionary of Spirituality*, entry on the Song of Songs, p. 356.
2. Quoted from Jacques de Vitry (1180–1254) in Colleen McDannell and Bernhard Lang, *Heaven, A History*, p. 98.
3. Quoted from Pope's commentary, p. 19.
4. In the following discussion, quotations from the Targum are taken from Pope's commentary.
5. The English translation cited is that by Lawson in the *Ancient Christian Writers* series. The discussion draws on an earlier publication, 'Sexuality and Devotion: Mystical Readings of the Song of Songs'.
6. *Commentary* I.2; Lawson, pp. 64–70.
7. *Commentary* III.2, on Song 1:16; Lawson, p. 173.
8. *Commentary*, Prologue; Lawson, p. 29.
9. *Commentary* III.8; Lawson, p. 198.
10. *Commentary*, Prologue; Lawson, pp. 38–9.
11. *Commentary* III.8; Lawson, p. 198.
12. As before, the ET cited is that of Marvin Pope.
13. I owe this point to David Ford, Regius Professor of Divinity in the University of Cambridge.
14. Cf. Chapter 3.
15. A point made by Robin Lane Fox in his book, *Pagans and Christians*.
16. A translation can be found in *NPNF*.
17. Chapters 1 & 2.
18. A translation can be found in *NPNF*.
19. A translation can be found in *ACW*.
20. See further my article, 'Adam, the Soul and Immortality'.
21. Verna Harrison, 'Gender, Generation, and Virginity in Cappadocian Theology'.
22. *On the Song of Songs* 11; ET Daniélou & Musurillo, pp. 246–8.
23. *On the Song of Songs* 4; ET Daniélou & Musurillo, pp. 178–9.
24. See the discussion of Rebecca Weaver, entry on 'Prayer' in *Augustine through the Ages. An Encyclopaedia* (ed. Fitzgerald).
25. *Ennarrationes in Psalmis* 41:8–9; ET in *ACW*.

INDEX

body 98, 101–2, 121, 125–6
bride 105–6, 109–12, 119–20
love 105–6
Otherness 92
passion 43, 53, 59, 65, 92
risen 41, 57, 91
temptations 55
theophanies 37–8
Way 58–80
Jews/Judaism 41–2, 45, 48, 51, 53, 63, 87, 93, 96, 103–4
Scripture/canon 77, 106–9
Job 28, 46–7, 53–4, 86, 114
John Chrysostom 6, 40
John the evangelist/John's Gospel 19, 21, 67, 78, 122–3
I John 118
John the Persian, Abba 3, 16
Jonah 22
Jonathan 96–8
Jordan 108
Joseph 22, 56, 90
journeying 17, 20–3, 25–6, 28, 30, 32, 35, 37, 100–1, 125
Justin Martyr 6, 38, 51, 62–3

katabasis 10, 118, 120
katharsis 10, 23
Kearney, P. 103–4
Keble, J. 114
kenosis 10, 16, 59, 67, 69–70, 72, 75, 78–9
King James Bible 115
Kings 123
Kosovo 28
Kotze, Revd T. 28

Lane, B. 25, 28

language 47–51, 93–5, 103, 106–7, 113, 116, 120
Last Supper 98–9
Latin 109
Latin America 87–8
Law 21–2, 108, 110
Leibnitz, G.W. von 45
Lent 23
Leo the Great 6, 38
liberation theology 87, 89
limitations 71, 77
Lisbon earthquake 44
liturgy 12, 23, 47, 73
Logos 10, 38, 103
Lourdes 57, 102
love 57, 59, 63, 67, 69, 73–4, 83, 85, 87, 100, 103–4, 106–8, 111–14, 116–24, 125–6
Luther, M. 37

Macarian Homilies/Macarius 6, 16, 56
Mamre 38
Manichees 7, 67
manna 12
Marcion/Marcionites 7, 67, 77
martyrs 60, 63, 65, 79
Mary Magdalene 41, 57
Mary, Virgin 112, 118, 121
Matter 51–2, 61
Matthew 21, 63
Mattins 13
Maximus of Tyre 7, 48
media 24, 29, 70
Mendips 123
Mephibosheth 11, 96–9
Merton, T. 27, 46
Messiah 108

metaphysics 113
Middle Ages 93
Middle East 82, 93
Midianites 90
Millenium 64
miracles 59, 62, 64, 74, 99
models 17–20
modernity 44–7, 53, 69, 77, 95, 123
monasticism/monks 14–17, 54, 56, 65, 115
Moses 17–22, 48, 56, 90, 108, 122
Moubarac, Father Y. 26
Mozart, W.A. 122
Muslims 28, 93, 104, 114
mysticism 17, 106
myths 63–4

Name of God 49, 57
nationalism 70, 82
nations 108
nature 71, 76, 112–17
Nazis 96
Nemesius 117
Neo-platonists 117
New Testament 13, 49, 54, 91
Newman, Cardinal J.H. 61
Noah 56
Northern Ireland 28, 93
Nuer tribe 95
Numbers 78

obedience 16, 21, 64, 68–9, 86, 122
Okavango Delta 71
Old Testament 37, 49, 76–7
oral tradition 36
ordination 101

Origen 7, 39, 55, 63, 109–13, 116, 119
orphans 89–90, 99
Orthodox churches 28, 47, 56, 82, 93, 101
Otherness 47–53, 59, 90, 92–4, 100–4, 125
Othona community 79
Othona Psalms 80–1
outsiders 82, 90, 101–2

paedagogus 11, 38
pagans/paganism 48, 63–4, 85, 87, 91, 115
Pakistan 93
Palestinians 104
parables 23, 50, 87, 93, 95, 107–9
Paradise 21
paroikoi 11, 91
Paul 16, 39, 41, 54, 66, 98–100
Peniel 35–6
Pentecost 78
perfection 17–18, 20, 74, 77
Peru 26, 55
Peter 16, 62, 91
Pharaoh 21–2, 90
philanthropia 11, 40
Philippe 72
Philippians 20, 59, 66–8
Philo 51
philosophers/philosophy 27, 48, 51, 63–5, 83, 87, 103, 115
physics 110, 113
Pietists 56
Pilate, Pontius 60, 65
pilgrimage 57, 62, 84–8, 92, 120–1, 125
Plato 7, 48, 51